SOCIOLOGY OF EDUCATION

SOCIOLOGY OF EDUCATION
An Introductory View from Canada

Joyce Barakett
Ailie Cleghorn
Concordia University

Prentice Hall Allyn and Bacon Canada
Scarborough, Ontario

Canadian Cataloguing in Publication Data

Barakett, Joyce, 1941–
  Sociology of education: an introductory view from Canada

ISBN 0-13-081035-5

1. Educational sociology—Canada. I. Cleghorn, Ailie, 1940– . II. Title.

LC191.8.C2B37 2000   306.43'0971   C99-931955-8

Prentice-Hall, Inc., Upper Saddle River, New Jersey
Prentice-Hall International (UK) Limited, London
Prentice-Hall of Australia, Pty. Limited, Sydney
Prentice-Hall Hispanoamericana, S.A., Mexico City
Prentice-Hall of India Private Limited, New Delhi
Prentice-Hall of Japan, Inc., Tokyo
Simon & Schuster Southeast Asia Private Limited, Singapore
Editora Prentice-Hall do Brasil, Ltda., Rio de Janeiro

ISBN 0-13-081035-5

Vice President, Editorial Director: Laura Pearson
Acquisitions Editor: Dawn Lee
Marketing Manager: Christine Cozens
Developmental Editor: Karen Elliott
Production and Copy Editor: Vicky Oskroba
Production Coordinator: Peggy Brown
Art Director: Mary Opper
Cover Design: MaryBeth MacLean
Page Layout: Carol Magee

  2 3 4 5   WEB   04 03 02

Printed and bound in Canada

Visit the Prentice Hall Canada Web site! Send us your comments, browse our catalogues, and more.
www.phcanada.com Or reach us through e-mail at **phabinfo_pubcanada@prenhall.com**

Contents

Chapter 3 The Organization of Teaching and Learning 46

Chapter 4 Critical Perspectives on the Politics of Teaching and Pedagogy 69

Chapter 5 The School as an Informal System of Socialization 92

Chapter 6 Education and Change 108

Preface

This book is written for undergraduate students who seek a sociological understanding of the educational process. It is especially written for students in education or sociology, who as future educators will need to be knowledgeable of current sociological debates in education in general and in Canadian education in particular. For this to occur, a knowledge of sociological concepts and theoretical perspectives is required in addition to an understanding of the ways in which the formal and informal aspects of the educational system are connected to the political, economic, legal, religious, and other sectors of society. It is of paramount importance that teachers and other educators develop the critical skills that will be needed if they are going to respond with good judgment to the constant pressures to introduce various changes, including the new technologies, into their schools. This book asks them to remember that education is essentially—and ultimately—about people and social processes.

Although the focus of this book is on the Canadian educational system, it is not simply a sociology *of* Canadian education. As the title suggests, we present a view *from* Canada. This is important for several reasons. First, we believe it is important to illuminate to the now highly multicultural student population, which includes many international students, what distinguishes Canada and its educational system from that of others. Second, we would like to convey that which is particular to the Canadian vision of *how society ought to be organized*, even if the reality may fall short of the vision. Here we have in mind what appears to us as a particularly Canadian way of looking upon ethnic, linguistic, racial, and other *differences* with a sense of the right of those differences to exist, to persist, and even to flourish. Although not everyone would agree with us, we believe that Canadians are in general agreement about the promotion of *unity in diversity* through the promotion of biculturalism, French and English bilingualism, and, wherever possible, through official support for the maintenance of other first languages. We would go further to suggest that most of the time Canadians are comfortable with the consequence of the foregoing: The necessity of negotiating mutual understanding in a civilized manner across multiple social boundaries.

In this book we draw on studies carried out in the United States, Britain, and France to show how the field of sociology of education has developed. From time to time, we also draw on far-reaching examples from various parts of the globe to locate the Canadian system within the broader context of issues, trends, and practices, and to help students take an objective stance towards their own system of education. Since people tend to take for granted the system that educated them, it can be difficult to see its components and effects clearly; many of the particulars have been internalized. To understand that which is familiar, it sometimes helps to take a look from afar. Therefore, although we have written this book with a Canadian readership in mind, it would make an equally useful text for American or British students, providing them with a different "world view," and thus illuminating their understanding of their own educational system and their experience within it.

The decision to write this book grew out of our combined experiences teaching sociology of education, comparative education, and gender and education courses at Concordia University. As instructors, we found that the few available Canadian texts soon went out of print, and we had little choice but to assign American or British texts or readers, none of which provided the perspective that we felt was necessary for understanding Canadian education in its broader context.

We know of no other current Canadian text that attempts, in the manner that this one does, to link theory and practice to an analysis of the controversial issues in education that affect the Canadian system in the context of a rapidly changing world. This book is a response to our concern that it is no longer enough to educate teachers for Canada alone. If their perspective is not broadened beyond their own borders they will not be prepared to adapt to and teach in situations where the school structures, rules, and expectations of teachers and students may be unfamiliar. Increasingly, these situations, as described in Chapter 3, exist in our own society and are also encountered when we travel to teach in other parts of the world. Thus we hope that this book reflects not only the range of historical and theoretical perspectives that affect education in Canada but also new ways in which educators can develop strategies for future educational and social change.

Probably every academic textbook purports to represent "the state of the art" in its field. We believe that this is best accomplished by signalling to the reader that some "old" ideas are fundamental to current thinking and, therefore, remain valid. State of the art means linking the best thinking in the field—no matter how old—as intelligently and coherently as possible to new thinking. It means avoiding faddist jargon, since this obfuscates understanding. It means drawing on our own considerable experience teaching at the university level and conducting educational research in Canada and elsewhere.

Guide for Instructors

This book is designed primarily to be used as the main text in a one-term, 12–14-week undergraduate course. Although it is organized into six chapters, we do not believe that any of these chapters can be covered properly in a single week. Rather, we recommend that you take about two weeks for the teaching and discussion of each chapter, especially if the suggested readings at the end of each are assigned in whole or in part throughout the course.

At the end of this book you will find a glossary of terms as well as a list of Weblinks. The glossary is intended to provide the reader with a quick reminder of the main idea of a concept or term; however, for a complete definition as applied to the field of sociology of education, the student will need to turn to the chapter in question.

The list of Weblinks represents a concession on the part of the authors to social and technological change. The intention is that these will be helpful and add to rather than detract from the knowledge provided in each chapter.

The table of contents reflects the overall aims of the book. The chapters are organized around major themes and are designed to clarify the relationship between school and society. That is, we show how the structures and the functions of societal institutions affect the educational process, and how the educational process, in turn, influences, transforms, or maintains these institutions. Further, the intention is to show how this process affects the education and lives of students. To make this text both interesting and meaningful, we have included illustrations, tables, case examples, and current Canadian data.

Chapter 1 provides the basic terminology and an introduction to the main concepts in the field of sociology of education. This chapter also discusses the structure of the Canadian educational system in terms of system goals and governance, showing how the Canadian system is either similar to or different from education systems elsewhere. The educational experience of Canada's First Nations people is then discussed along with a brief look at minority rights in education. The chapter ends with an introduction to sociological research in education.

Chapter 2 provides a historical overview of present-day thought in the field, then reviews the major theories that have been put forth to explain the nature of the relationship between schooling and society.

Chapter 3 looks at the organization of teaching and learning in terms of the formal organizational features of the school. It includes a discussion of the norms of the teaching profession and the roles of teachers as well as that of the principal. The question of whether or not there is a crisis in teacher education is examined in the context of trends in teacher education in Canada. This discussion is followed by an overview of current and past models of teaching. The chapter ends with a section on curriculum, including curriculum debates and curriculum as process.

Chapter 4 distinguishes between teaching and pedagogy through a discussion of critical and feminist pedagogy and the politics of education. In this chapter, we show the influence of the work of Paulo Freire.

Chapter 5 provides the reader with an overview of the role of the school as an informal system of socialization. Here the student will gain a more thorough understanding of the meaning of the hidden curriculum, which was introduced in Chapter 1.

Finally, Chapter 6 looks at education in Canada today in the context of change. Several critically important ideas and issues are raised for future teachers and educators to give serious consideration to as we move into the twenty-first century.

As much as possible throughout the book we have tried to indicate how the various theories, first mentioned in Chapter 1 and then fleshed out in subsequent chapters, apply to each and every topic under discussion. Thus by the end of the text the reader should have a clear understanding of the link between theory and practice.

To assist you in an appropriate plan for using this book, a suggested course outline is available from your Prentice Hall sales representative.

Acknowledgments

Many people have helped, directly and indirectly, with this book. First to be mentioned are the hundreds of students we have taught, especially in sociology of education, comparative education, and gender and education courses. We have drawn many lessons from them in designing a book that would be both readable and informative.

Second, we want to thank several people for their individual contributions. Judith Leonard and Deborah Baverstock-Angelus, now both graduated from Concordia's Educational Studies masters program, very kindly gave of their time and energies to go back to their theses and contribute to the inserts on The Alternate School in Chapter 4 and the use of teacher narratives in teacher education in Chapter 3. Annie Potter, a Concordia doctoral student in the Special Individualized Program, contributed to the section in Chapter 6 on inclusive education. She also set us straight when the language we used ceased to communicate. Lucie Lalonde and Amanda Benjamin, both Concordia masters students in Educational Studies, helped with the typing and worked on the references when they got out of control. And Douglas Scott, a computer technician in the education department, came often to the rescue when computers refused to cooperate.

We are also grateful to the following people, who have reviewed some or all of this manuscript: Rodney A. Clifton, University of Manitoba; Amarjit Singh, Memorial University of Newfoundland; Deborah Boutilier, Brock University; Eva Krugly-Smolska, Queen's University; Kim Lutton, University of Western Ontario; Arlene McLaren, Simon Fraser University; and Jarrold Kachur, University of Alberta.

Many people at Prentice Hall have helped us see this book to completion. Particular thanks are offered to Karen Elliott, Dawn Lee, and Vicky Oskroba.

Finally, thanks to our colleagues and families for their "lots of luck" encouragement.

About the Authors

Joyce Barakett is associate professor in the education department at Concordia University. Her doctoral degree is from the Université de Montréal and is in Sociology of Education, Social Psychology, and Sociology of Women. She has a B.A. from Concordia University and an M. A. in Sociology from McGill University. Her courses include undergraduate and graduate teaching in Sociology of Education, Gender and Education, School and Society, and the Social Implications of Technology in Education.

Ailie Cleghorn is associate professor in the education department at Concordia University. Her doctoral degree in the Comparative Sociology of Education was completed at McGill University in 1981. She holds a B. A. from McGill University in Sociology and Anthropology and an M. A. from Concordia University in Educational Studies. She teaches undergraduate courses in Comparative Education. At the graduate level, her courses include Literacy and Development and Minority Status and Learning. Her research has focused on language issues in second language classrooms in Kenya, Zimbabwe, and Montreal.

SOCIOLOGY OF EDUCATION

THE NATURE OF SOCIOLOGICAL INQUIRY AND THE STUDY OF SCHOOLS:

The Scope of the Field

Chapter Objectives

The objective of this chapter is to provide an understanding of the major concepts in the field of sociology of education. This is done primarily with reference to the functions of education. The structure of the Canadian education system is then outlined so that the student can see how it is both similar to and different from other systems around the world, especially in terms of system goals and governance. The chapter ends with a brief introduction to the topic of sociological research in education, showing how problems may be approached from different methodological perspectives.

SOCIOLOGICAL CONCEPTS

By the time students are in their third or fourth year of university they have come to realize that the educational system that they have been exposed to over the previous 15 or so years is complex, but few really understand how complex and in what ways. It is, therefore, our purpose to provide you with an understanding of the ways in which educational systems, structures, and processes connect with various aspects of society, including dominant values, political goals, and ideologies. To understand the scope of the field of sociology of education we must first define some basic terms. Before we move on to the sociology of education, we need to have a clear understanding of what the field of sociology is.

Sociology is a social science discipline which explores and explains the organization and functioning of society. It is a field of study that looks at the social groups (social classes, ethnic, linguistic, and racial groups) and institutions that make up a particular society. By institutions we are referring to the family, the economy, the legal, and the political systems. Sociology is also concerned with the relations between the social groups as well as the position or status of the individual within the group, groups, or institutions that he or she belongs to. The ideologies that underlie the functioning of society's institutions, as well as the values, norms and beliefs of society's various groups, are a major part of the field of sociology.

Sociology of education is a subfield of sociology with two major foci. At one level it focuses on the relationship of schooling processes, practices, and outcomes to the organization of society as a whole; at the level of the school system and within the school itself, it focuses on the social groups (teachers, students, parents, school administrators, school board officers, ministry of education), the relations between them, and the academic as well as social results of in-school processes. Sociology of education is thus particularly concerned with such matters as the manner in which educational processes ensure, for example, that individual students come to abide by the norms and values of society at large, and the role that the educational process plays in recreating society's social structure as this relates, in particular, to the division of labour and the hierarchy of power.

To further understand sociology of education we need to distinguish between the kind of everyday or **informal education** that normally takes place within the family (starting at birth) from formal education, which takes place in institutions (schools) designed for that purpose. **Formal education** refers to the set of organized activities that are intended to transmit skills, knowledge, and values as well as to develop mental abilities. We can also talk about **nonformal education,** which refers to organized instruction that takes place outside of school settings (e.g., girl scouts, music lessons, sports groups). Our main interest in this book is with formal education within regular school settings.

Education is sociological because it is part of a network of interrelated societal institutions, because it is a **social process,** and because of its functions, both intended and unintended. That is, education takes place within an established institutional structure (a school system) which is connected to other institutions in society—the economy, the political system, the legal system, and the family, as well as the belief or religious system. The dominant norms and values of society are reflected in all of these institutions.

Education is also a sociological process at another level. It involves human beings and requires them to interact in order for the intended knowledge, skills, and values to be transmitted, and for mental abilities to be developed. The main participants in this process—the teachers and the students—bring to the classroom their prior life experiences, their **social class** background (a combination of parents' education, occupation, and income), their language background, their racial origins, their gender, their beliefs about each other and about education, and their notions of how girls and boys are supposed to behave in classrooms. What goes on in classrooms is, therefore, greatly influenced by these factors or variables, or, more accurately, by the social meaning that is attached to such matters as language, ethnicity, race, and gender.

It is important to note that some school settings are more complex than others with regard to the variables just mentioned. For example, because of large numbers of immigrants, especially since the end of the Second World War in 1945, schools in major cities in Canada are now very multicultural and multilingual, as they are in other countries such as the United States, Britain, and Australia. This **diversity** of the student population makes it more important than ever before for teachers to be educated and prepared for the experience of teaching children who may bring to the learning situation many different kinds of prior experiences stemming from their varied social class, language, and cultural backgrounds. In turn, these differences will mean that in any single classroom children can be expected to vary considerably in their learning styles, attitudes towards school, and expectations regarding the roles of teachers and students. Thus it is not only the **social context** of teaching and learning that is important, but the context of the experience that each child brings to school. To *contextualize* instruction is to attend to both of these aspects of the culture of schooling.

The Functions of Formal Schooling

The functions of schooling can be categorized as either **intended** (manifest) or **unintended** (latent), though there is considerable overlap between the two. The unintended functions of education are also considered to be part of what is known as the hidden curriculum (Mifflen & Mifflen, 1982).

Intended Functions of Schooling

By intended or manifest functions we are referring to those aspects of schooling which come immediately to mind when we ask ourselves what it is that schools do. It seems simple at first. As already stated, schools transmit knowledge, skills, and values and develop mental abilities. Apart from the other obvious fact that elementary schools do different things than universities, is this all there is to it? Let us look first at four intended functions of schooling.

1. Schools transmit generalized as well as specialized knowledge.
2. Schools transmit the existing culture from one generation to the next and to new members of the society.
3. Schools transmit new knowledge that is produced in universities and in industry.
4. Schools provide opportunities for social mobility.

To elaborate on the first (the transmission of generalized and specialized knowledge), we teach children to read, write, and to calculate, that is, to be **functionally literate**, providing them with the general knowledge they will need to take part in society, to work, and to learn other things. At a more specialized level, we teach many facts in subjects such as history, geography, art, music, and literature, as well as procedures in subjects like science and mathematics. Nowadays we teach computer and other skills that will be useful in specific jobs. These are the kinds of obvious things that come to mind when we ask what it is that schools do. The situation is not so simple, however, when we begin to ask *whose* knowledge is taught in school, and *who has decided* what is to be taught at what level, *to whom*. We will return to these important sociological questions later.

What do we mean when we say that schools transmit the society's existing culture (the second function mentioned above), including the accumulated knowledge and the dominant values, from one generation to the next and to new members of the society? By **culture** we are referring to the ways of perceiving, thinking, believing, and behaving that characterize the members of a particular social group. Culture also includes the artefacts that distinguish one group from another (e.g., clothing, technology, type of housing). In complex, multicultural settings the transmission of culture through the school is not a simple, straightforward matter because of the multicultural make-up of many classrooms. That is, the culture that is being transmitted in school reflects the values and attitudes of the so-called **dominant group.** We are referring to those (mostly men) who hold key decision-making and leadership positions in society as well as those who are closely associated with them, professionally or through friendship. This includes those who are in charge of the school system. Sometimes the dominant group's culture differs in important ways from the home culture of many or even most of the students. Thus we see that schools play not only a socialization role from one generation to the next but also a role in the acculturation of the children of newcomers (immigrants) to the norms and values of the dominant society. **Acculturation** refers to the changes that occur within a group through culture contact and through the process of adapting to and taking on the values, attitudes, and ways of behaving of the culturally dominant group. Some refer to this as the process of integration.

Culture contact occurs when members of more than one culture or ethnic group live in proximity to each other. The group that arrived first or has been in the region the longest tends to include those who hold the important and powerful positions in the society's institutions (including the school system).

Although Canadian law includes provisions for religious and ethnic minorities to establish their own schools, it is generally the culture of the dominant group that is transmitted through the public schools. In this way, cultural transmission involves acculturation. By bringing together young people from various backgrounds within a single societal institution for a number of their formative years, schools play an important role in establishing loyalty and consensus over what the society most values (i.e., a sense of national identity or citizenship). In some countries schools promote national loyalty overtly, with daily saluting of the nation's flag, for example. In countries such as Canada acculturation tends to be more subtle, contained within federal multicultural policies, which are in turn expressed through school festivals that celebrate diversity.

Cultural transmission also involves **cultural diffusion**. For example, Western culture, values, and schooling practices, including curricula, have been spread or diffused to communities in the Canadian North as well as to many parts of the still-developing world through colonization and its aftermath. Cultural diffusion also refers to the dissemination throughout society of new knowledge that is produced in universities as well as in industry. Cultural diffusion may be increasing globally through the textbook industry, which tends to be controlled by Western capitalist interests (Apple & Christian-Smith, 1991).

Cultural production refers to the role that higher education institutions play in producing new knowledge in technology, science, the social sciences, the humanities, business, art, and other areas. Through a complex decision making and implementation process, new knowledge is incorporated into the school curriculum. In due course, it is passed on to the next generation and to new members of the society (Werner,1987).

Before proceeding to discuss the social mobility function of the school, it is important to clarify what we mean by social structure. **Social structure** refers to the way people's relations in society are organized to form patterns or networks. The social structure of complex societies like Canada is made up of multiple systems or institutions—the economic, political, family, religious, and education systems. From a **functional perspective**, the societal structure may be compared to a living organism that is basically stable. Temporary stresses may move the society away from equilibrium, but this tends to be short term, with stability being returned to quite "naturally." According to this view, social mobility takes place within an established social structure or network of personal and institutional relations where people occupy different statuses and roles. The persistence of inequality, therefore, is considered, in the overall, functional for the society as a whole, though not for individuals.

In contrast, from a **conflict perspective** inequality is considered as dysfunctional for the society as a whole, and as something imposed by those in positions of power through institutional processes that may well be taken for granted by most people as simply the "way things are" (Mifflin & Mifflin, 1982). Functional, conflict, and other theories will be discussed more fully in the next chapter.

Every society, from the smallest and most simply organized to the large and complex (such as Canadian society) is stratified, or has a system of **social stratification**. That is, every society is organized in a hierarchy based on people's access to and possession of whatever is most valued in the particular society. Individuals (and the groups they belong to) are accorded prestige and power (status) based on such matters as education, income, occupation, race, ethnicity, religion, language, and gender. Canadian society is stratified on the basis of ethnic and linguistic background, occupation, education, and income (Porter, 1965). That is, the system is stratified according to both **ascribed status** and **achieved status.** While the Canadian system of stratification is considered to be "open," allowing movement up through the strata, from the lowest to the highest on the basis of achievement, the extent to which such **social mobility** is actually possible is still limited by ascription (characteristics one has at birth such as gender, ethnicity, and social class). In other words, there are limits, albeit ill-defined ones, on the extent to which achievement in school can compensate for ascribed characteristics: academic achievement tends to be patterned by ascribed characteristics, although individual exceptions can often be found.

A society's system of stratification is also related to the **division of labour**, the differential distribution of jobs that need to be done in order for the society to maintain itself economically. Every society has unwritten rules as well as formal criteria (the required credentials) that determine who may perform which tasks. The unwritten rules are generally based on such matters as gender, ethnicity, family background and the like. And every society has some tasks that are considered more important or more desirable than others. Similarly, some occupations are more highly valued than others and pay accordingly. Since it is not possible for all qualified people to perform highly desirable tasks, there has to be a selection process. In fact, some theorists would argue that there has to be a way for a society to ensure that achievement is distributed unevenly (patterned). There also has to be a way for people to accept their lot. We must ask, then, How is it that people "accept their place" and agree to perform even the most menial of tasks? How do individuals get ahead? How is the system of social stratification perpetuated?

In Canadian and North American society in general, we find a widely held belief that schools are places for people to acquire the credentials that will allow them to move up the social ladder. It is widely believed that there is **equality of educational opportunity** (equal access to schooling, equal treatment within schools, and the potential for equal results). This is a popular but ill-defined concept, and more of a myth than a reality. If educational opportunity were truly equal for all there would be no differential distribution of educational results: achievement would be distributed evenly from one social class to another, from one racial and ethnic group to another, and between the sexes. While not all people are equally able to achieve well in school, there is no evidence whatsoever to suggest that some individuals are more intelligent than others based on their social class, race, ethnicity or gender. That is, there is no biological or genetic reason why one group or another should be overrepresented among either those who succeed or those who fail in school (Ogbu, 1991; Slavin, 1991).

In addition, there is a related set of myths stating that those who achieve well in school have done so through hard work, and by being evaluated according to objective and "fair" (universalistic) principles. Most people prefer to believe that a family's social class, racial origin, language spoken at home, or other particularistic criteria do not affect a student's performance in school. This is to say, there is a popular belief that we live in a **meritocracy**, where individual effort and ability lead to higher achievement in school and, therefore, to higher social status. As we shall see later on in this text, this also is more myth than reality. At this point, it is important to understand that myths serve the important function of building and maintaining consensus and social cohesion, but that this comes at a cost to individuals who are members of certain groups (Aronowitz & Giroux, 1993).

The same set of myths or beliefs is used to explain why some students fail in school, take up menial jobs and do not move up the social ladder. To take this reasoning a bit further, if girls fall behind boys in mathematics, there must be a good reason for it; if special education classes are made up of a disproportionate number of children from minority backgrounds, there must be a good reason for this also. This kind of commonsense understanding or belief that justifies or rationalizes the way things are, and thereby supports the status quo, is called a **legitimating ideology**.

Although the majority of people have enough intelligence to achieve quite well in school and to perform a variety of occupations, there is some truth in the fact that not all individuals are equally suited to a given task. In addition, the distribution of jobs to be done does not necessarily match the distribution of abilities. There are fewer interesting and prestigious jobs than there are intelligent people. Thus there has to be a way to select some to perform certain kinds of roles and to persuade others to perform low-status jobs. This process is part of the **selection and allocation function** of schooling. Although manifest and intended at one level, the selection-allocation function of schooling is difficult for many to see, since we have all been socialized to believe that the system is fair and just. It is for this very reason, however, that it is extremely important for teachers to know about this function of schooling. It is one of the main concerns of the field of sociology of education.

Closely related to what we have just said about social mobility is the fact that through the process of schooling young people learn a lot about the occupational structure of society. Schools introduce young people, both directly and indirectly, to many occupations as well as the types of position and roles within them. For example, children learn early about the hierarchy of power when they find out that serious infractions (both behavioural and academic) get referred "up the line" to the principal of the school. Similarly, they learn that there are complex rules associated with competition, cooperation, and achievement; sometimes chatting in groups in the classroom is cooperative learning, other times chatting in class is considered disruptive behaviour. In such ways children eventually become familiar with society's rules for getting ahead, with what constitutes fair competition, with what counts towards academic achievement, and what does not. Thus, through observation of repeated patterns of interaction between all the actors in the school—the principal, the teachers, the librarian, parent volunteers, the janitor—children are introduced to occupational roles. They also discover who has authority over whom and what kind of behaviour is acceptable under what circumstances. It is through such mechanisms that children also come to accept the results of tests which are said to be objective, and, therefore, fair. The belief that testing procedures are unbiased and fair is an important precursor to later acceptance of the fact that the rewards of society are distributed unevenly—some people get ahead and "deserve" to, while those who do not can only "blame themselves." We will discuss this legitimating ideology in more detail in Chapter 2.

Unintended Functions of Schooling

There are several functions of schooling that are considered unintended, or less obvious and recognized than the preceding intended or manifest functions. We will discuss four: (1) social control; (2) custodial; (3) establishment of social relations and subgroup maintenance, and (4) promotion of critical analysis. (See Mifflen & Mifflen [1982] for a more complete discussion of manifest and latent functions.)

Social control is not only about the control of undesirable behaviour; it is about the definition and imposition of the expected behaviours of boys, girls, Blacks, whites, teenagers, university students, and so on. Social control refers to the role that the school plays in perpetuating social class differences; it refers to the unwritten rules that define who is expected to get ahead and who is not. These are the rules that sometimes result in subtle or not-so-subtle rejection of an individual who "steps out of line," by showing an interest in entering an occupation that requires years of higher education despite, for example, the modest educational achievements of his or her parents. These are the rules that lead some girls to suddenly lose interest in science or mathematics at about the age of puberty and other students to rebel against the system in ways that conform to popular racial or ethnic stereotypes (Dei, 1996; Ogbu, 1991). The functional theorists, who will be discussed more fully in the next chapter, would say that it is through social control that the social structure is maintained in a kind of equilibrium.

Schooling can also be said to have a **custodial function**. This refers to the fact that elementary schools, at least, are places for children to be looked after, to be guaranteed the same safety they enjoy at home, from about nine o'clock in the morning until at least three o'clock in the afternoon. Nowadays many elementary schools recognize the importance of their custodial role by providing care for children during parents' working hours, from early morning until late afternoon. The custodial function of schools is reinforced through a variety of laws which place a legal responsibility on the school and on teachers to substitute for parents (*in loco parentis*) during the school day (Dickinson, 1995). They are held responsible for the safety and care of the child, but, interestingly, schools are not (yet) legally responsible when children fail academically: failure belongs to the individual and can easily be explained according to the myth and belief system discussed above.

The custodial situation in high schools is not quite so clear. While schools may have a legal responsibility to provide a safe environment for young people, this does not always happen. In fact, some high schools are dangerous places for students and teachers alike—drugs, violence, rudeness, defiance, and truancy appear to be increasing everywhere.

We realize how important schools are for developing social skills and establishing social relations when we imagine children learning everything they need to know at home in front of a computer. Not only do children learn at school how to get along with their peers and to work in groups, but, by virtue of their location in residential neighbourhoods, schools tend to draw children from similar social classes and ethnic backgrounds. Over time, the friendships that develop become part of a community's adult network of social relations, reinforcing and maintaining the cohesion of particular ethnic, linguistic, social class, and other subgroups within the society.

It may be another myth that schools teach students to think critically about the society they live in as well as about global issues. While there are a few reports of experiments in high schools to promote critical analysis (Norris & Phillips, 1990), it appears that very little instruction in critical analysis actually occurs until the graduate level of university. It is important, therefore, for sociology of education students to think about why it is that critical thinking is so rarely encouraged at earlier stages of schooling.

While elementary and most secondary schools are quite conservative institutions, they are also places where social changes are felt and technological changes are tried out. Thus one of the functions of higher education is to carry out research, and to reflect on the changes occurring in society and how these changes affect the educational process. Schools now have to deal with many different kinds of change, such as a vastly increased divorce rate (deemed a problem by most teachers), immigrants who adhere to religious practices that are unfamiliar to members of the host society, and computers, which are being adopted as a new panacea for every conceivable educational problem. These are but a few of the changes that require study, critical reflection, and consultation with teachers, teacher educators, school administrators, the education ministry, and others. These are also the kinds of issues that academics take up in sociology of education courses with preservice teachers and others interested in the field of education.

THE CANADIAN EDUCATIONAL SYSTEM IN AN INTERNATIONAL CONTEXT

University students may not initially realize what is different about the Canadian educational system, or, alternatively, in what ways it is similar to other systems throughout the world. In this section we will try to paint a broad picture of how the Canadian system is located according to a number of factors that tend to vary from one educational system to another.

Educational systems vary worldwide in many ways, but some of the more obvious differences relate to structure, governance, goals, and historical influences (Thomas, 1990). Structure refers to the formal organization of schooling: the number of years allocated for primary education as well as the number of years of secondary education. It refers as well to the presence or absence of any formalized preschool such as kindergartens, as well as the total minimum number of years that school attendance is compulsory. **Governance** refers to the way the education system is controlled and operated.

Structure and Governance

Canada's system of education is unique in terms of governance. At a national level it is highly **decentralized**, while within each of the ten provinces it is **centralized**. This means there are ten systems of education in Canada, in addition to the three education systems in each of the territories (Northwest, Yukon, and Nunavut), which until recently were controlled by the federal Department of Indian Affairs. The territories now have their own equivalents to education ministries; however, funding of their school systems is still federal. Each of the ten provincial systems normally allocates six or seven years for primary schooling and five or six years for secondary schooling. Most elementary schools contain kindergartens, although these are not legally mandated, and attendance is not compulsory.

In Canada we have universal access to elementary and secondary schooling and we require by law that young people remain in school until the age of 15 or 16 (about grade 9), depending on the province. This is not the case everywhere; there are many countries that do not yet provide universal access to elementary schooling and many countries that do not have laws requiring children to attend school. This being said, there is no lack of demand for formal schooling throughout the world. Parents everywhere want their children educated; however, when faced with economic constraints, parents everywhere tend to educate their sons for longer than their daughters (Gordon, 1997; Lindsay, 1990; UNICEF, 1994).

Figures 1–1 and 1–2 outline the basic structure of the Canadian education system showing that there is minor variation from one province to another. For comparative purposes, Figures 1–3 and 1–4 provide an overview of the Italian education system. While the Canadian systems provide a similar secondary education for all, through grade 11 in Quebec and grade 12 in the other provinces, the Italian system provides 6 different institutional tracks after grade 8 (about age 14). Other interesting differences in education structures may be observed in the education systems of Japan, Russia, Germany, and France, for example (Thomas, 1990).

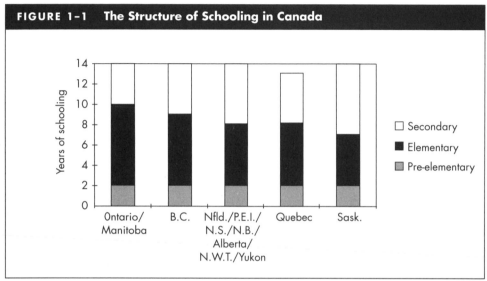

FIGURE 1-1   The Structure of Schooling in Canada

Source: Adapted from Organization for Economic Cooperation and Development (1996).

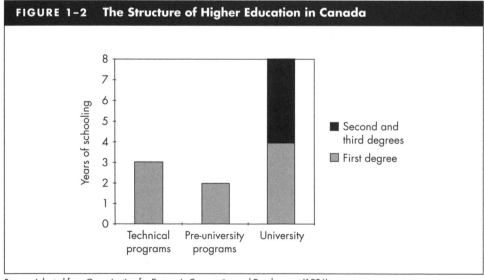

FIGURE 1-2   The Structure of Higher Education in Canada

Source: Adapted from Organization for Economic Cooperation and Development (1996).

Another factor that varies from one country to another is the length of the school year. Table 1–1 shows that the length of the school year varies from a reported 251 days in China to 172 days in Portugal, with Canada's average being 185 days. Recent cross-national stud-

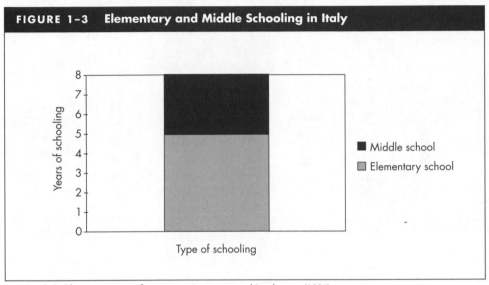

FIGURE 1-3   Elementary and Middle Schooling in Italy

Source: Adapted from Organization for Economic Cooperation and Development (1996).

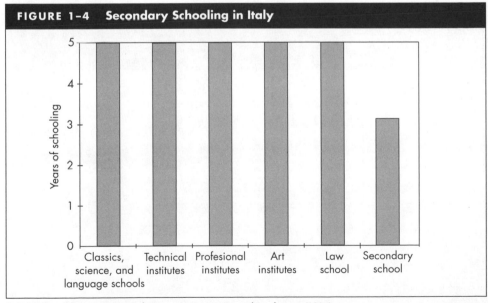

FIGURE 1-4   Secondary Schooling in Italy

Source: Adapted from Organization for Economic Cooperation and Development (1996).

ies of educational achievement do not suggest, however, that performance in mathematics or science, for example, is significantly related to the length of the school year (Orpwood & Garden, 1998). Other factors such as teaching strategies are more important.

TABLE 1-1	Length of School Year in Various Countries	
Country		**Days**
China		251
Israel		215
Switzerland		207
Italy		204
England		192
Canada (average)		185
United States		178
France		177
Portugal		172

Source: Adapted from international comparisons from a selected sample from National Center for Education Statistics, Washington, D.C., for 13-year-old students. As reported in the *Globe and Mail*, April, 1994.

Another way to compare education systems is to look at the length of the school day. While this factor varies considerably across Canada, as Figure 1–5 shows, there is little, if any, evidence to suggest that differences in the length of time spent in school are reflected in achievement. Again, it appears that achievement is more closely tied to the subtleties of

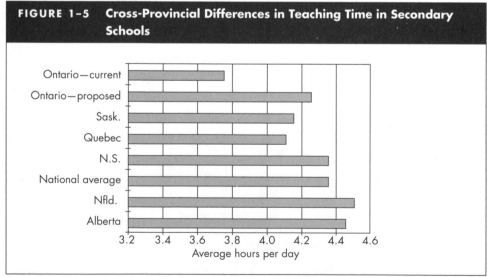

FIGURE 1–5   Cross-Provincial Differences in Teaching Time in Secondary Schools

Source: Adapted from international comparisons from a selected sample from National Center for Education Statistics, Washington, D.C., for 13-year-old students. As reported in the *Globe and Mail*, April, 1994.

how things are done in classrooms, rather than how much time is spent there (Stigler & Stevenson, 1988/89).

Although Canada has 13 different and legally separate systems of education, there is a remarkable similarity across the country from one system to another. What is taught by the end of primary school in New Brunswick is sufficiently similar to what is taught by the end of primary school in British Columbia to allow a child to move from one part of the country to another, normally without losing ground. This suggests that there is a considerable degree of consensus in Canada about what children ought to be taught at which grade level, as well as about how they should be taught. Such consensus is not cross national. If a child were to move to any part of Canada from an impoverished education system in a still-developing country, the child would likely be far behind her or his peers in some subjects, but especially in the ability to learn without relying on rote memorization. Similarly, should a child move to a Canadian province from Japan or Singapore, for example, she might find herself ahead of her age-mates in some subjects (Stigler & Stevenson, 1998/99).

The governance of different education systems can also be studied and compared. It is important to ask *who organizes* the system*, who controls it,* and *how* it is controlled. Where does Canada fit into the range here? While the majority of countries have highly centralized systems of education, there is still much variation, and the trend internationally is towards decentralization. The educational system in France is among the most highly centralized, while the system in the United States may be the most decentralized. Canada lies somewhere in the middle.

Under the terms of the British North America Act of 1867 (now called the Constitution Act), education falls under the control of the provinces and territories, not the federal government. While the Canadian federal government deals with issues relating to the equalization of funding for education between the provinces, all other aspects are dealt with at the provincial level. Each province and territory has its own Ministry of Education that oversees matters relating to the organization of school boards, parent involvement in school management, curriculum, examinations, teacher education, and teacher certification.

By contrast, in the United States, for example, the role of the federal government in education is being eroded by increasing pressure for local control, driven by an ideology that favours less government interference in the life of the family and the individual. Interestingly, this ideology coexists with a form of nationalism that places much emphasis in the schools on the establishment and perpetuation of national identity and loyalty. In Canada, the promotion of nationalism plays a less obvious—if not inconsequential—part in the schooling process.

Educational Goals

Most industrialized countries today have a national system of education that has been influenced historically by Europe, England, or the United States. In the late eighteenth and nineteenth centuries, education was seen as a way to ensure politically friendly relations between different countries (i.e., to reduce the risk of war), especially as it was primarily reserved for the political elite. For national development purposes, the state controlled schooling. Control of educating the masses was thus taken away from local elites, from churches, and from families, with the capitalist class creating a system that would serve their need for compliant workers. It was only by the end of the nineteenth century that universal, public systems of education were established in the Western world, while attempts were made to implant similar systems in the colonies of Africa, Asia, the Middle East, and Latin America. These attempts were more or less successful for the elite of those countries, but less so for the masses, mainly because of the nature of global economic and political relations, persistent poverty, and restricted curricula (Thomas, 1990).

When we speak of **educational goals** we raise a complex set of issues. As Thomas (1990, p. 25) discusses at length, societies do not vary greatly in terms of stated general goals, but they do vary in regard to the more specific goals. These are most often tied closely to the society's economic conditions and needs. Educational goals are also influenced by historical events such as wars and by the sequel to natural events, such as the discovery of oil in the Middle East. Educational goals vary depending on which institutions in the society have responsibility for defining the goals (e.g., the family, the church, and the state). They also vary in terms of the manner in which decisions are made about which learners may pursue which goals. For example, before the system of apartheid was dismantled in South Africa in 1995, Blacks were not permitted access to certain schools and universities; what was offered in the schools designated for Blacks virtually excluded them from a quality education, from certain occupations, and from full participation in the society as a whole.

Statements about general educational goals often refer to such matters as producing good people who are faithful citizens with the ability to take part in their community. When we examine the specific goals, however, we see that these reflect very different views of the learner. In some parts of the world, the emphasis is on the memorization of large amounts of factual material due to the orientation towards and importance of national examinations. These examinations, normally held at the end of the primary cycle (grade 6, 7, or 8, depending on the country) determine an individual's chance for further education and, therefore, the individual's life-long occupational opportunities. In other regions of the world, including most of the West, the emphasis is on teaching children how to learn, how to study, how to judge what they read, and so on.

Closer examination of these differences reveals that they may be related to the number of available spaces at the secondary or university level. When there is a shortage of spaces at the next level of schooling, one often finds a national examination system, deemed to be fair and objective, that allows the system to select the number of students for whom there are spaces at the next level. It is important to note that the number of available spaces at the next level determines the cut-off point (the failure point) in examination results. The definition of failure has little to do with what the children have learned; it simply identifies the few who can be absorbed into the next level of the system.

One consequence of this situation is that there are huge numbers of people in some countries who must live with an artificially defined and externally imposed sense of failure. In the case of some African countries, where economic conditions created serious shortages of spaces at the secondary level and beyond, there was a need to select about one-third of primary school leavers for whom there were available spaces at the secondary school level. For the remaining two-thirds, their education ended at the primary level. This situation persists in some countries, is worsening in others (such as Rwanda and Zambia), and is improving in South Africa. In Canada, we have no need for such an all-important examination system because there is no shortage of spaces at any level of the system; however, as we shall see later, Canada is still far from providing the same educational opportunities for everyone. The discussion of a seemingly straightforward matter such as educational goals thus quickly raises a number of issues connecting an education system to economics, politics, and the dominant values of the society in which the system is rooted.

Education of Canada's First Nations People

Canada's population has become especially diverse since the end of the Second World War. But Canada has always been diverse; its diversity, however, was not fully acknowledged and, until the last 20 years or so, it was somewhat invisible to many Canadians. In fact, today there is considerable public controversy over the national belief that there were "two founding peoples," the English and the French, for the aboriginal peoples have been here longer than anyone really knows. This is, in short, the story of colonialism throughout the world.

Colonization is also the story of the way that involuntary minority groups are formed. That is, when people immigrate to a country they may become members of what some have identified as **voluntary minority** groups because, with the exception of refugees, it is assumed that leaving their countries was intentional and that they hoped to change certain aspects of their lives. However, as Ogbu (1991) and others have pointed out, the educational experience of these two types of minority groups has tended to be very different, with involuntary minorities generally being treated harshly, in a racist manner, or even with segregation, as witnessed by the system of apartheid in South Africa and the creation of native reserves in North America.

We are beginning to see the aboriginal peoples of northern Canada, Australia, New Zealand, Greenland, Scandinavia, and South Africa take charge of their own communities, land, welfare, and schooling as well as relations with their political counterparts in the respective federal governments. While the education situation of Canada's native peoples is still in flux, there is much that can be said about it. A brief historical outline will suffice for the moment.

Traditional education of aboriginal peoples was nonformal, oral, and adapted to the economic survival needs of the group. Early formal education in Canada was carried out by missionaries whose goals were to convert the native people to Christianity and to rid them of the cultural and linguistic traditions that the missionaries found so strange and threatening. The aim was total control. This was accomplished by the nineteenth century by isolating native children in residential schools, forcing a European curriculum on them, denying them their beliefs and language, and, eventually, by severing them from close family relations (Barman, 1987; Cardinal, 1977) .

The results of nearly three centuries of inappropriate schooling are well known (Cardinal, 1977). The damage is only beginning to be repaired, mostly by the people themselves. Cultures disintegrated, languages disappeared, and traditional ways of ensuring survival have been replaced by guns and skidoos. Nonformal, oral ways of transmitting indigenous forms of knowledge were taken over by a definition of knowledge which values only that which is written down in books. The consequence of these long-standing circumstances has been a very high drop-out rate and few adults with formal high school leaving certificates (Fletcher, 1999). At the start of the twenty-first century about 28 percent of the aboriginal population living on reserves have less than grade 9 education compared to about 5 percent of the total population. About 11 percent of the total Canadian population have a university degree, while 1 percent of on-reserve aboriginal peoples have a university degree (Statistics Canada, 1993).

This situation has been improving as the number of band (Indian)-operated schools have increased since the 1970s. Increasingly, these schools use appropriate curricula, specially trained teachers (including more and more aboriginal teachers), native languages for instructional purposes wherever possible, and a school year adapted to the hunting and fishing economy.

Regarding the Inuit of the Northwest Territories and now the newly formed territory of Nunavut, residential schools were designed to undermine their cultural values, and federally operated day schools were part of the effort to settle the Inuit into permanent communities. Mandatory schooling introduced a totally new set of values into the North, and disrupted seasonal family hunting patterns as well as the authority of the family. As a result, for many Inuit today, schooling is a mixed blessing. On the one hand, there are many shared, bitter memories; on the other hand, schooling is now seen as necessary to future survival. Although things are changing, most of the teachers are still from the "south" and not fully able to compensate for culturally embedded differences in learning styles (Lipka, 1991; Stairs, 1991). The curricula and teaching materials are still not fully relevant to life in the North. Ways still need to be found to establish comfortable bicultural competencies.

The situation in the territory of Nunavut, formed in April 1999, shows considerable promise. Nunavut was formed out of about two-thirds of the Northwest Territories. The majority of the people in the local government are Inuit, and they, along with some imaginative Inuit teachers, have had a major hand in the planning of the education system. Due to the increased number of native teacher training programs at Canadian universities, there are now many native teachers in the primary schools. The number of native teachers at the community-based high schools is also beginning to rise. The general goal is to enhance Inuit culture and language through an adapted Alberta school curriculum with a strong science core, which includes indigenous knowledge and indigenous perspectives. Since there are suddenly numerous new white collar, administration and construction jobs to support the new Nunavut government, there is now evident logic in completing trade school or high school. In addition, the first venture into post-secondary education has begun with Arctic College. Arctic College has agreements with several universities in the south to launch and staff a number of innovative programs including a transitional, pre-college, pre-university bridging program, and an executive Masters in Business Administration, offered by St. Mary's University in Halifax (Fletcher, 1999).

While never a justification for inhumane treatment of an entire people, it is important to understand that the goals of those in charge of the education of the First Nations and Inuit people were tied to economic considerations, namely the fur trade, gold mining, fishing, and logging. These were all activities that, at the time, seemed to require having control over the native peoples' land and resources. Thus, we see how easily economic considerations become political considerations, which are then reflected in educational practice (Jaenen & Conrad, 1993).

Minority Rights

We cannot leave this section without mentioning the right that the Canadian government affords to its linguistic and religious minorities to establish their own schools. These rights were first established under Section 63 of the BNA Act of 1867 and later reaffirmed in the 1982 Canadian Charter of Rights and Freedoms (Ghosh & Ray, 1995). Under the law, each province must provide a public (free) education for the Protestant as well as the Catholic majorities, though not necessarily in separate school systems, or even in separate schools, and religious and ethnolinguistic minorities have the right to establish private, fee-paying but government-subsidized schools. In Quebec, due to the historic coupling of religion and language, a dual system of public education has evolved which is, in fact, divided four ways: French-Catholic with a small French-Protestant sector and English-Protestant with a small English-Catholic sector. Since 1977 and the passing of Quebec Bill 101 (the French Language Charter), French became the sole official language of instruction in the province, with a small minority of English-speakers who had attended English schools in Canada retaining the right for their children to be educated in English. All others were henceforth to attend French-medium schools (Ghosh & Ray, 1995).

While the language laws of Quebec may seem strange, as educational sociologists we would argue that their strangeness lies primarily in the tacit assumption that the position of the English-speaking majority of the country ought to prevail, despite the facts that education is under the control of the provinces and the majority language group in Quebec speaks French. When one considers that French, as spoken in North America, is a language at risk of dying out, the measures of Bill 101 make sense. In addition, until the mid-1960s, the English-speaking 20 percent of the province's population were a numerical minority but a sociological majority in terms of their power in the society, especially in the business sector. With the Quiet Revolution in the 1960s, there came a collective push on the part of many French-speaking people to be "masters of their own house" (maîtres chez nous). The result was a series of new language laws, the most important being the 1977 Bill 101. We will return to this topic in Chapter 6.

RESEARCH IN SOCIOLOGY OF EDUCATION

Who carries out research in sociology of education? What questions are explored and how? What are some of the unresolved questions of the field? Are there new questions arising with emerging social problems and issues? Are there new directions in research that could be or need to be taken? How are the results of studies analyzed and used? Who benefits from the research?

Sociologists of education are interested in exploring questions relating to several main issues in education. Some of the issues are located at the **macro level,** where society at large and education connect. For example, researchers want to know why it is that *inequality* in society is perpetuated through the process of schooling, and they want to know as precisely as possible what the mechanisms are for this occurrence. It is only with such understanding that solutions can be proposed.

Other issues that are investigated are located **mid level**, at the level of the school and the social relations that occur within the school (Martin, 1976). What, for example, is the nature of the social relations between French- and English-speaking students in Canadian schools where both groups are found, and do these relations reflect the long-standing separation between the groups in society at large? (Cleghorn & Genesee, 1984). Still other research concerns are **micro level** in focus. Here, for example, one might ask if teachers interact with and use speech differently with different types of learners. One might also ask whether the discourse patterns in different language settings differ, for example, in native Canadian classrooms as contrasted with non-native classrooms (Crago, Annahatak & Ningiuruvik, 1993). When questions like these are explored in careful, systematic ways, we add to what is known about the optimal learning conditions for different kinds of learners.

All these questions ultimately may contribute information to the ways that schools do or do not create equitable conditions for learning. In due course, we understand better how to maximize the opportunities in schools and classrooms for equality of access to education, equality of treatment within the school and classroom, *and* equality of results. We are not implying here that everyone has a right to the same results, simply that everyone has a right to be schooled in conditions that allow each child to reach her or his own potential.

What methods do educational sociologists use to explore the kinds of questions just mentioned? It depends on both the questions being asked and the way that the researcher conceives the nature of social reality. Stated differently, it depends on the theoretical and methodological perspectives of the researcher.

Theoretical and Methodological Perspectives of the Researcher

There are several theoretical perspectives adapted from the field of sociology for use in the study of educational issues and problems. To oversimplify for the moment (more detail will be provided in Chapter 2), education can be seen from a functional perspective, as contributing to the overall equilibrium and stability, or status quo, of a society. In this view of social reality, the education system replicates the social structure of society as a whole, including the world of work; the norms, the hierarchy, the system of rewards, the organization of schools and classes are all geared to recreate the social system much as it is. Change occurs slowly and without disruption.

Alternatively, the conflict theorist views social reality as unstable: in a state of conflict and disequilibrium. The education system is looked on as a system of power and control, perpetuating intergroup conflict, including the oppression of minorities. Conflict theorists see the status quo as likely to persist unless there is a concerted effort to bring about change, through strikes and other kinds of social upheaval.

In contrast to the conflict theorists, **interpretive theorists** (sometimes called humanists, interactionists, or phenomenologists) do not view social reality as concrete, but, rather, emphasize the need to study educational systems in terms of the meaning that events hold for those who participate in the process. This perspective is, therefore, subjective. According to this view, society emerges from and is maintained by social interaction, in spite of the structural constraints on this process. Change is seen as occurring through the actions of individuals, most often acting as members of groups. That is, change is seen as occurring from the grass-roots level of society rather than simply imposed from above.

While additional theories will be discussed in Chapter 2, this brief thumbnail sketch simply lets us see that there are several ways of looking at the process and effects of schooling. These different ways of looking underlie the kinds of questions that researchers who align themselves with one perspective or another are likely to ask. For example, a functional theorist might ask how the educational system is supported by society's political, legal or economic systems. A conflict theorist might be interested in the power relations between the different groups within the formal and informal organization of the school. In turn, the researcher who holds to an interpretive perspective might want to know how teachers and students "negotiate" the social order of the classroom, or what meaning the different groups in a school attach to the same events (Martin & McDonnell, 1978).

Just as social reality can be analyzed from a number of theoretical perspectives, educational research, too, can be conducted from one of two major, but divergent, **paradigms**, or stances. One is **quantitative**, the other **qualitative**. These two paradigms, which are, in fact, not opposites but mutually supporting, represent long-standing differences in research approaches. The quantitative approach stems from the positivistic tradition of the so-called pure sciences; the qualitative approach stems from the humanistic tradition of the social sciences.

When we identify a research problem, frame research questions, and decide how to carry out the study, we draw upon our way of seeing the world, our theoretical perspective. That is, we use a paradigm. Paradigms are characterised by differing sets of assumptions about the phenomena to be studied. Each paradigm includes a set of assumptions about the nature of social reality, about what constitutes a legitimate research problem, about the purposes of research, about the nature of truth, and about the relationship between the researcher and the research subjects. Researchers often disagree about the validity and reliability of the knowledge that is produced from each perspective. Researchers who adhere to the quantitative paradigm tend to rely for proof on statistical analysis of results, while qualitative researchers are more comfortable with subjective interpretations of events offered by both the research subjects and the researchers.

Some researchers see the schooling process in terms of inputs and outputs **(independent and dependent variables)** that can be counted. The reasons for variability in examination results, for example, can be determined through statistical analysis and manipulation of the input (independent) variables through **controlled experiments**. The number of hours of instruction, for example, might be correlated with test results in one classroom where the hours of instruction have been experimentally altered. The results would be compared to those of another class (the control group) where no change has been made. Such studies are concerned with **cause and effect**.

Other researchers see the schooling process as laden with human values, as heavily influenced by the interaction between home, school, and personal variables, and as affected by the interplay between the various interpretations of schooling events. In the eyes of the qualitative researcher, to try to determine cause and effect through quantification is to reduce the social reality of schooling to a compilation of numbers. After looking at the differences between these two approaches (see Table 1–2 for a summary), we will look at how they can be integrated.

TABLE 1-2 Comparison of Quantitative and Qualitative Research Perspectives	
Quantitative	**Qualitative**
• assumes social reality is stable	• assumes social reality is dynamic
• seeks facts or causes	• seeks understanding of human behaviour
• outcome oriented	• process oriented
• viewpoints of subjects are irrelevant	• viewpoints of subject are relevant
• results are decontextualized; a representative sample of the population studied	• results are context bound (holistic), sample not necessarily representative of the population
• objective, the researcher removed from the data	• subjective, the researcher is involved and close to the data
• experimental or quasi-experimental	• exploratory, descriptive
• uses obtrusive, controlled methods of data collection	• uses naturalistic, unobtrusive methods of data collection
• deductive—tests hypotheses and makes inferences from data	• inductive—raises hypotheses for further inquiry
• statistical analysis; results are reliable, valid, and can be generalized	• many sources of data; totality of situation reconstructed from perspective of the subjects; findings are particular, cannot be generalized
• theory testing	• validity comes from richness and depth of data
	• theory building

Source: Adapted from Bogdon & Biklan (1992).

Although many sociological studies in education conform to one perspective or the other, we believe that the most suitable approach to most problems and issues in education is one that combines the two, although this may be time consuming and costly. Ideally, the researcher should begin a study with a *tentative* or general set of questions or hypotheses about an issue, perhaps based on existing theory. Presuming, for purposes of illustration, that the problem being explored has something to do with what goes on in classrooms, the researcher would then spend several weeks or months carrying out classroom observations to get a better understanding of the complexity of the issue. At first, the observations would be broad in scope, and would slowly become more focused and systematic as the researcher gained familiarity with the setting. The researcher would then analyze the observational data for consistent patterns and raise specific hypotheses for focused study. At some point, the researcher would raise highly specific hypotheses that would suggest the need for a controlled or experimental study, and the ensuing data would be analyzed statistically. The results would then be interpreted according to statistical conventions *and* in light of the subjective observational data. At this point, it would be appropriate to return to the classroom for further observation, and, possibly, for discussions of the results with the teachers and students. Their views of the situation being studied would then be incorporated into the final interpretation (the theory building stage) of the data.

Several theoretical perspectives and their relationship to the kinds of questions that educational researchers ask have been mentioned briefly in this chapter. In the following chapter, these theories and their origins will be discussed in detail so that we can understand the prevailing ideas about schooling and society.

SUMMARY/CONCLUSIONS

In sum, the scope of the field of sociology of education is broad. Sociologists of education are concerned with multifaceted issues that may be broken down into a multitude of interrelated parts. We are able to understand the issues and to devise solutions to persistent educational problems, both locally and abroad, due to the large amount of research that has been conducted and continues to be conducted in this field.

This chapter has provided the reader with the formal terms and vocabulary that will be needed to discuss and write about topics in sociology of education. We have tried to stay away from jargon and to indicate as clearly as possible that some of the terms may have two sets of meaning: an everyday meaning and a more abstract sociological meaning. We hope that these terms will become useful tools for expressing complex ideas, both inside and outside the university setting.

The chapter has also given an overview of the structure and goals of the Canadian educational system, including a brief account of the history of education of Canada's First Nations people.

Although the section on research is brief, it is intended to be comprehensive enough for students to grasp the main idea that there are different ways of looking at issues and problems in education. An understanding of the different research perspectives is necessary to identify the various components of an education problem and then explore it in detail.

KEY TERMS

acculturation	controlled experiments	custodial function
achieved status	critical analysis	decentralized system
ascribed status	cultural diffusion	dependent variables
cause and effect	cultural production	diversity
centralized system	culture	division of labour
conflict perspective	culture contact	dominant group

educational goals

equality of educational
opportunity

First Nations people

formal education

functional perspective

functionally literate

governance

in loco parentis

independent variables

informal education

intended functions

interpretive theorists

legitimating ideology

macro, mid and micro
levels of analysis

nonformal education

qualitative paradigm

quantitative paradigm

selection and allocation
function

social class

social context

social mobility

social process

social stratification

social structure

unintended functions

voluntary minority

DISCUSSION QUESTIONS

1. What does this chapter tell you that you did not know before about the educational system that you went through?

2. Using some of the terms from this chapter, explain to a friend or the other members of a class group what you think was particular about your own schooling experience.

3. Select an educational problem that is sociological in nature. List all the aspects of the problem that you can think of. Suggest a feasible plan to explore the problem.

RECOMMENDED READINGS/REFERENCES

Anderson, G. (1990). *Fundamentals of educational research*. New York: Falmer Press.

Apple, M. W., & Christian-Smith, L.K. (Eds.). (1991). *The politics of the textbook*. New York: Routledge.

Aronowitz, S., & Giroux, H. (1993). *Education still under siege*. New York: Bergin & Garvey.

Barman, J. (1987). *Indian education in Canada*. Vancouver: University of British Columbia Press.

Bogdon, R. A., & Biklan, S. (1992). *Qualitative research for education: An introduction to theory and methods*. Boston: Allyn and Bacon.

Cardinal, H. (1977). *The rebirth of Canada's indians*. Edmonton: Hurtig.

Cleghorn, A., & Genesee, F. (1984). Languages in contact: An ethnographic study of interaction in an immersion school. *TESOL Quarterly, 18*(4), 595–625.

Crago, M., Annahatak, B., & Ningiuruvik, L. (1993). Changing patterns of language socialization in Inuit homes. *Anthropology and Education Quarterly, 24*(3), 205–223.

Dei, G. (1996). Black/African-Canadian students' perspectives on school racism. In M. I. Alladin (Ed.), *Racism in Canadian schools* (pp. 42–57). Toronto: Harcourt Brace.

Fletcher, C. (1999). Nunavut EMBA Information package. Department of Anthropology. St. Mary's University: Halifax.

Ghosh, R., & Ray, D. (Eds.). (1987). *Social change and education in Canada* (1st ed.). Toronto: Harcourt Brace.

Ghosh, R., & Ray, D. (Eds.). (1995). *Social change and education in Canada* (3rd. ed.). Toronto: Harcourt Brace.

Gordon, R. (1997). Structural adjustment and women in Zimbabwe: Effects and prospects. *Canadian Journal of Development Studies, XVIII* (2), 263–278.

Jaenen, C., & Conrad, M. (1993). *History of the Canadian peoples.* Mississauga, Ontario: Copp, Clark, Pitman.

Lindsay, B. (1990). Educational equity in cross-national settings. In M. Thomas (Ed.), *International comparative education: Practices,issues, and prospects* (pp. 197–226). New York: Pergamon.

Lipka, J. (1991). Toward a culturally based pedagogy: A case study of one Yup'ik Eskimo teacher. *Anthropology and Education Quarterly, 22,* 203–223.

Magnuson, R. (1980). *A brief history of Quebec education.* Montreal: Harvest House.

Martin, W. B. W. (1976). *The negotiated order of the school.* Toronto: MacMillan.

Martin, W. B. W., & McDonnell, A. J. (1978). *Canadian education.* Scarborough, Ontario: Prentice-Hall.

Mifflen, F. J., & Mifflen, S. C. (1982). *The sociology of education: Canada and beyond.* Calgary: Detselig.

Norris, S. P., & Phillips, L. M. (1990). *Foundations of literacy policy in Canada.* Calgary: Detselig.

Nunn, E. J, & Boyatzis, C. J. (1998/99). *Child growth and development.* Guilford, Connecticut: McGraw-Hill.

Ogbu, J. U. (1991). Low school performance as an adaptation: The case of Blacks in Stockton, California. In M. A. Gibson, & J. U. Ogbu (Eds.*), Minority status and schooling* (pp. 249–286). New York: Garland Publishing.

Organization for Economic Cooperation and Development (1996). *Education at a glance: OECD Indicators.* Paris: OECD.

Orpwood, G., & Garden, R. A. (Eds). Assessing mathematics and science literacy. *TIMMS Monograph Series #4.* Vancouver: Pacific Educational Press.

Porter, J. (1965). *The vertical mosaic.* Toronto: University of Toronto Press.

Slavin, R. E. (1991). *Educational psychology:Theory into practice.* Engelwood Cliffs, New Jersey: Prentice Hall.

Stairs, A. (1991). Learning processes and teaching roles in native education: Cultural base and cultural brokerage. *Canadian Modern Language Review, 47(*2), 280–294.

Statistics Canada. (1993). *Aboriginal data.* Document 94-327. Ottawa: Statistics Canada.

Stigler, J. W., & Stevenson, H. W. (1998/99). How Asian teachers polish each lesson to perfection. In E. J. Nunn, & C. J. Boyatzis (Eds.), *Child growth and development* (pp. 90–101). Guilford, Connecticut: McGraw-Hill.

Thomas, R. M. (Ed.). (1990). *International comparative education: Practices, issues and prospects.* New York: Pergamon.

UNICEF. (1994). *Children and women in Zimbabwe: A situation analysis.* Harare.

Werner, W. (1987). Curriculum and socialization. In R. Ghosh, & D. Ray (Eds.), *Social change and education in Canada* (1st ed.) (pp. 91–101). Toronto: Harcourt Brace.

Chapter

THEORIES OF SCHOOLING AND SOCIETY

Chapter Objectives

The intent of this chapter is to provide an overview of the dominant theorists and to briefly summarize the most important perspectives (theories or paradigms) that sociologists use to explain the relationship between school and society. We draw on these theories to explain various aspects of the schooling process in later chapters. In addition, we critique each approach and present its limitations.

ORIGINS OF SOCIOLOGY OF EDUCATION

Present day thought in sociology of education has been informed by the writings of mid-to late-nineteenth century sociologists and social philosophers. The works of classical sociologists and social philosophers such as Karl Marx, Max Weber, Emile Durkheim, and George Herbert Mead are most important in understanding schooling and its relationships to other social and economic forces in modern life. Although none of these founding "fathers" of sociology wrote extensively about education, they are important because their political ideologies influenced the development of sociology of education in Europe, and later, in Canada and the United States.

Karl Marx's (1818–1883) political ideas have shaped history in many ways and persist in doing so. Born near the border between Germany and France, Marx was the son of a Jewish lawyer who converted to Christianity to avoid persecution. In Germany, Marx studied philosophy and German; later in Paris and Brussels he studied economics.

Deeply affected by the living conditions of workers in Europe, he sought to explain capitalism theoretically and to fight it politically. He wrote his more important works in London, where he moved to escape hostility due to his political views and activities. Marx believed that the economic organization of a society is central to its class structure, institutions, cultural values, and beliefs . At the core of his theory is the belief that the economic base of a society, that is its mode of production, determines the "social, political and spiritual processes of life." More specifically, he argues that the way people earn their living profoundly affects how they think, how they relate to others, and, most significantly, how they relate to the structure of society and culture. This has come to be known as economic determinism.

For Marx, socialism (ownership by workers of their society's factories, land, and other productive assets) would follow capitalism (private ownership of the means of production) as the final stage in the evolution of history and politics. This change would occur only after a social revolution. The importance of Marx's thought to the field of education can be seen in present day theories relating to the question of power and how those who are in important positions in economic and political institutions control the structure of the educational system. For example, in Canada it is the Ministry of Education of each province which controls the curriculum in elementary and secondary schools, while both provincial and federal governments allocate funding to the schools.

Emile Durkheim (1858–1917) focused his studies on social order and used statistics and empirical methods to explain the forces that he believed made social events regular and predictable. Born in Eastern France, the son of a rabbi, Durkheim's major contribution to social theory was his analysis of social integration, social control, ritual, and the moral base underlying society, all of which he said make social order possible. For instance, Durkheim saw schools as key institutions that provide moral unity through forging a sense of nationhood and a commitment to common values and beliefs, and creating cohesion or social integration.

He was interested in the societal mechanisms that account for the maintenance of social order as well as in the deviant aspects of that order. For instance, he focused on what he perceived as the societal causes of suicide, looking at patterns of suicide among different social classes and groups. He was one of the first to note that personal difficulties such as depression and school failure can be linked to economic conditions and other societal processes.

Max Weber (1864–1920), born in Germany, the son of a wealthy German politician, wrote on many subjects—religion, economics, politics, authority, bureaucracy, class and caste, and the city. Like Marx, he was interested in explaining the rise of capitalism; however, unlike Marx, he believed that systems of ideas, including religions, influence economic behaviour, not the reverse. He also believed that understanding people's actions through the meanings of their own and others' behaviour must be of primary concern for the sociologist. Weber's primary objective was to acquire a causal explanation for social action. Questions he posed were derived from broad situations such as the historical interplay of Protestantism and capitalism. He analyzed historical and comparative data to show that religious or cultural ideas are not only the result of, or solely dependent upon, economic factors alone. Weber maintained that materialistic factors played an important role in the rise of capitalism but that the ideas and belief systems that make capitalism possible should also be considered. That is, we must consider the "spirit" of capitalism, generated from hard work, thrift, and the willingness to use profits for new investments and expansion. He argued that Puritan Protestant sects (Protestant ethic or Calvinism) are an excellent example of this "spirit." His data demonstrates that modern capitalism emerged where these beliefs and ideals were present.

His analysis proceeded from the construction of theoretical **ideal types,** which he used to interpret historical events and actions and to create causal explanations. For example, he studied complex formal organizations or bureaucracies in terms of ideal types that are founded on the characteristic institutions in the basic organizations of the society. Another of Weber's major contributions was his analysis of **status groups**. Status group is used to describe people who share a social identity based on similar values and lifestyles. For instance, members of the same status group may belong to the same social clubs and participate in similar social activities. We will see later how theorists use this concept to explain inequality in educational opportunity.

In contrast to the social, economic, and political concerns of the European sociologists, North American philosophers and social theorists were beginning to analyze the nature of social reality from the perspective of the individual, the individual being a member of a group, and groups being the constituents of a society.

In the 1920s, through the work of sociologists at the University of Chicago (also known as the Chicago School of Sociology), a new perspective, referred to as **interpretive sociology**, was developing. These sociologists were primarily concerned with the perception of the nature of self and social interaction. Among the most prominent in this school were Charles Horton Cooley, W. I. Thomas, and George Herbert Mead. Cooley's (1864–1929) theory of the origin of the self centered on the *looking-glass effect*. By way of the looking-glass metaphor, Cooley illustrated that individuals, through interaction with parents, peers, and teachers, come to see themselves as they imagine others see them. W.I. Thomas (1863–1945) presented us with the concept of the **definition of the situation**, suggesting that if we define a situation as real, then it becomes real in its consequences.

Mead (1863–1931) incorporated Cooley's and Thomas' insights but also went on to state that self-development and self-awareness require the capacity to use language and interact symbolically. Symbolic interaction involves individuals responding to objects, situations, and events according to the meanings that these have for them. Symbolic interaction will be explored in further detail in Chapter 5. Furthermore, he argued that to interact with others the individual must *take on the role of the other*, that is, to imagine how this other views him, and to know what this other expects. Mead believed that individuals act and react to one another according to these mental interpretations. Mead's concept of **self** includes the **me**, a part of the self that represents internalized societal attitudes and expectations. The self also contains the **I**, a unique and emancipated part that produces spontaneity and individuality. These societal and individual aspects of the self collaborate to form an interactive quality he called *interactionist*. More will be presented on these theorists in the discussion on socialization in Chapter 5.

THEORIES OF SCHOOLING AND SOCIETY

Various sociologists, in their search for basic knowledge about schooling and their desire to explain the common assumptions about what schools actually do, drew on many of the concepts put forth by these ground-breaking figures in sociology. The following describes the sociological perspectives that were developed to explain the educational process.

Functionalist Theories

The functionalist perspective was one of the first theories that arose to explain the salient features of a developing industrial society. The 1950s brought immense technological advances in North America, a large influx of immigrants, and a population movement from rural to urban areas. A concern with social order and maintaining social equilibrium, ideas grounded in Durkheim's work on social integration and the moral basis of society, became of primary importance. Functionalists viewed dramatic changes due to the industrial revolution as also affecting the occupational structure. From this perspective, the expansion of higher education was important to ensure a literate society that could fill job requirements. This expansion, seen as necessary for the maintenance of social order, was linked to a deep-seated commitment to capitalism.

The functionalist view, then, became a source of explanation and justification for the role of schools in maintaining the organization of society in what was perceived as equilibrium. The role of schools was to teach the necessary skills and norms for the individual to participate in society, by sorting, selecting, and training people for jobs at each level in society.

This perspective is perhaps most clearly reflected in the works of Talcott Parsons (1967), James Coleman (1966), and Robert Dreeben (1968). They viewed the classroom as a social system, socializing and allocating individuals on the basis of the criteria, beliefs, and values accepted by the dominant group in society. The school's function was seen as dictated by and central to the economic and occupational structure of a developing modern industrial society. They were concerned with how differentiation of status occurs on the basis of achievement. The assignment of differential rewards to various positions in the status hierarchy is seen as a necessary technique to motivate talented individuals to achieve high status positions. From this perspective, education offers greater opportunities for attaining higher social status for those who can master the system.

To summarize, functionalists argue that schools socialize individuals by teaching norms, values, and skills to make them functional in society. Schools prepare individuals to meet the needs of the occupational structure. Functionalists are concerned with social stability and do not address the need for social change; they ignore the social class origin of individuals and its effect on school achievement. This then begs certain questions: Does the educational system serve the democratic or the technocratic needs of industrialized society, and does higher education increase equality of opportunity?

Some Canadian Functionalist Sources

The most important work that reflects the functionalist perspective in Canadian educational research is that of Guy Rocher and Pierre Bélanger (1975). Their analyses are based on the political situation in Quebec during the 1970s. They were concerned with developing a general theoretical framework for a sociology of education that would explain the educational and cultural revolution in Quebec.

Murphy (1979) notes that Rocher and Bélanger turned to a systems model of social action based on the works of Talcott Parsons to explain the relationship between school and society. They viewed society as a complex organism, which can be analytically divided into separate institutional structures such as the family and education, and into socioeconomic, political and religious divisions. To maintain a state of equilibrium, change in one of these institutions would inevitably create change in the others. For Rocher and Bélanger, education was one form of social action; education could transmit symbols, values, and rules of behaviour necessary to the maintenance of a stable social order. Rocher and Bélanger's concept of social action consists of four systems that are at the same time separate and interconnected. These systems are biological, personality-based, social, and cultural. Each system has its *functions* (needs or prerequisites of interconnected institutions) that are essential for the system to exist. Thus, the school system can be analyzed by these functions. For example, we can analyze the school as a subsystem of the larger society in relation to other subsystems such as the economy and political structure. These are the most basic aspects of Rocher and Bélanger's general theory, which they proposed for a sociology of education. There are rich analyses in their work and we urge students to read their writings.

John Porter is another important Canadian sociologist who reflects the functionalist perspective. His major work, *The Vertical Mosaic* (1965), some argue, points to the functionalists' concerns because he, too, views society as an organism consisting of interrelated subsystems. Unlike most functionalists, however, he points to the importance of power. Porter points to the tension that exists between the meritocratic and technocratic features of society, and it is this tension between the meritocratic and technocratic aspects of society that leads to a power struggle among the dominant power groups. For Porter, educational institutions exist to meet the needs of technological change and the occupational requirements of society. However, he emphasizes how the dominant power groups or the elites who control wealth, power, and prestige monopolize and manipulate higher education.

Wallace Clement (1975) replicates Porter's work on elites and discusses how elite groups maintain power through elite education, that is, by teaching the values and beliefs of those who are in power. His primary concern is to show how private schools and elite universities socialize the elite and restrict others through the promotion of dominant class values and beliefs (Mifflen & Mifflen, 1982, p. 73).

Conflict Theory and Neo-Marxist Theory

In the 1970s, a controversial debate developed about intelligence and school achievement , and the relationship between schooling and the future economic status of students. Collins (1977), a **Neo-Marxist theorist**, and others argued against the basic assumptions of the functionalists. He notes that society is not in a balanced state: Competition and the struggle between groups for power, wealth, and prestige is instead the normal situation. According to these theorists, functionalists support the status quo by stating that society is fine the way it is. Thus, conflict theory is grounded in the assumption that whenever one group gains, another group loses. The question is: Who dominates whom?

Collins refutes the notion that job skill requirements have increased due to technological advances, and that formal education provides the training necessary for upgrading job skills. He states that the main contribution of education to economic productivity occurs at the level of transition to mass literacy; better educated individuals are not necessarily more productive, and, furthermore, most skilled manual labourers learn on the job. Collins turns to Weber's concept of status and suggests that schools teach **status culture**, a particular lifestyle—language, dress code, peer association, and interests—that is deemed desirable by the dominant group in society. Students who learn this status culture will be more successful in achieving a higher social status. Collins notes that there are also distinctions among status culture groups based on ethnicity and class. These groups struggle for wealth, power, and prestige. Schools are controlled by powerful groups, which provide near exclusive education for high status culture groups, and, consequently, education becomes a means of cultural selection. Collins notes that a conflict theory of education must focus on two things: the struggle between status culture groups, and how status culture is learned in school.

Pierre Bourdieu (1977), whose work is referred to as the Cultural and Social Reproduction Theory, adds another dimension to status culture. He views education as a significant social and political force in reproducing the class structure of society. Bourdieu argues that the language and texts used in schools reflect the interests, values, and tastes of the dominant power groups. In this way, he creates a link between class, power, and education. The children of the elite acquire style, tastes, and language through "inheritance"; these higher status groups transform their **cultural capital** into academic capital. Because children from the lower class do not possess the cultural traits of the elites (they have different linguistic skills than those prescribed by the school, for example), it appears "natural" to sort them into lower streams that offer a different or less demanding curriculum. This streaming has led to the establishment of two different school systems, public and private, distinguished by the type of ability demanded of their students. Bourdieu explains that acquiring cultural capital in the form of educational (or academic) capital depends on families possessing strong cultural capital and transmitting cultural rewards to their children. Thus, cultural capital is a key mechanism in the reproduction of the dominant culture through which educational and social inequalities are perpetuated (Bourdieu, 1986). Bourdieu notes a second form of capital, *social capital,* which is "the aggregate of the actual or potential resources which are linked to possession of...institutionalized relationships of mutual acquaintance & recognition" (1986, p. 248). Social capital consists of "connections," which determine how effectively the individual uses his or her social capital.

Basil Bernstein (1973) argues that the explanation of social class differentials in educational achievement lies in the role of language in the primary socialization process. For him, social class has a great influence on this socialization process. His study of the British working class and middle class indicates that different forms and techniques of socialization affect educational achievement. He notes that in early socialization working-class children's forms of speech (vocabulary, grammatical by stem content) are typified by a "restricted code." For example, the working-class mother, when she controls her child, places less emphasis upon language, and deals only with the immediate action in a particular context rather than, say, by relating that action either to general principles or to the consequences of that action.

On the other hand, children of higher status groups are socialized into the "elaborated code," which gives them access to knowledge through general principles and orients them towards universalistic orders of meaning. Since schools operate within the "elaborated code", children from higher social classes have an advantage. Thus Bernstein conceives of the working-class child as deprived of something (the "elaborated code") that the middle-class children have as a result of early socialization. However, we can argue that working-class culture is just as complete and valid as middle class culture. Furthermore, Bernstein speaks of working-class and middle-class groups, each with their forms of socialization, language, and class as if these groups are homogeneous.

In the 1970s a controversial debate developed about the links between intelligence, school achievement, and the future economic status of students. Bowles and Gintis (1976), in particular, challenged the functionalist perspective and some of the concepts put forward by the conflict theorists. They argued that IQ scores, occupational status, and income are positively correlated. However, when socioeconomic status is controlled, IQ does not have an extensive effect on either future earnings or occupational status. Rather than concentrating on how students go about constructing meanings in classroom interactions, Bowles and Gintis focus on the school's role in reproducing the class system and extending the capitalist mode of production. They refer to this process as the **correspondence principle or theory.** They state:

> The hierarchically structured patterns of values, norms, and skills that characterize the work force and the dynamics of class interaction under capitalism are mirrored in the social dynamics of the daily classroom encounters...Schools, through classroom relations produce students that are docile and complacent—characteristics required in the workplace. (Bowles & Gintis, 1976, p.131).

They argue that the political process, through powerful economic interest groups, determines the role of education in reproducing and legitimizing social and economic inequality. Indeed, for them the root of inequality is the capitalist economy, not education. They claim that schools reproduce and legitimize inequality by

- perpetuating and reinforcing the meritocratic ideology of allocating individuals in the occupational hierarchy;
- rewarding personalities which are compatible with the relationships of dominance and subordination; and
- serving the interests of the dominant groups through the training of an elite group in the skills of domination (1976, pp. 11–13).

Bowles and Gintis' theory has been referred to as Neo-Marxist because it emphasizes that the values and power of the economic structure determine the nature of the social order, and therefore, the inequalities therein.

The following are some strengths and weakness of Bowles and Gintis' correspondence theory that have been noted by several authors. First, their theory shows that schools cannot be analyzed as institutions removed from a socioeconomic context. The correspondence theory posits a class analysis of schooling, one which shifts the blame for educational failure from teachers, students and school resources to the structural dynamics of the dominant society. Indeed, it points to how education contributes to the reproduction of the social order. Second, their theory does not show clearly that the correspondence between school and economic change is determined by capitalism. Third, some authors have questioned their emphasis on capitalist knowledge as the only knowledge produced in schools. Finally, Bowles and Gintis tend to provide us with a possible view of students that does not acknowledge contradictions and tensions that exist between schools and the workplace.

Some Canadian Contributions to Conflict and Neo-Marxist Theory in Education

Various articles in books edited by George Martell (1974) and Randle Nelsen and David Nock (1978) provide a critical analysis of how schooling in Canada is integrated into the corporate world under capitalism, and how post-secondary education effects class inequalities by imposing corporate values (for example, by emphasizing profit making in the curriculum). Studies in works edited by Livingstone (1983, 1985) and Wotherspoon (1987) point to how the Canadian educational system has become ingrained with class-based educational ideologies and practices.

Symbolic-Interactionist, Interpretive, and Phenomenological Perspectives

The **symbolic-interaction** model, produced by the Chicago School of Sociology, attempted to link social structural realities, such as wealth, power, and status position, with patterns of interaction. In other words, the symbolic interactionists attempted to understand how structural variables become incorporated into the individual's perceptions and interpretations and how the individual acts on the basis of these interpretations. According to them, the important point is that to understand social differentiation in educational settings, we must first understand how teachers categorize and classify various student behaviours. The assumption they make is that education is indeed related to social inequality. To understand how schools perpetuate inequality, we must learn more about the basic rules or **interpretive procedures** teachers use when interacting with students and with each other in an educational setting.

By examining student performance in the context of different types of questioning, researchers have demonstrated that low performance is not necessarily due to a lack of understanding of language and culture, rather it is the form of interrogation and the context within which it occurs that affects performance. Accordingly, we cannot assume that meaning is arrived at or transmitted in an obvious process. The interpretation of meaning, definitions, and the recognition of rules are all "developmentally and situationally constrained." That is, students and teachers, while interacting, respond to each other by reflecting, selecting, and then trying out a response on the basis of their social knowledge and the situation in which they find themselves.

Caroline Persell (1977) links *structural variables* such as politics and the economy with students' and teachers' interaction patterns to explain inequality in education. She explains inequality by showing how the dominant ideology of power groups penetrates four levels— societal, institutional, interpersonal, and intrapsychic. (A more detailed analysis of dominant ideologies and teachers' differential expectations is provided in Chapter 5.) At the societal level, Persell draws on Marx and Weber to point out how **structures of dominance** and the ideologies associated with these structures are interdependent. The institutional level (the structure of the educational system), then, is shaped by the polity and the economy. The schooling process—achievement testing, ability grouping, and tracking—reflects the structural needs of society.

By drawing on George Herbert Mead's symbolic-interactionist theory Persell then goes on to describe the interpersonal and intrapsychic levels. Here the focus is on the origins and consequences of teacher expectations. Teachers develop expectations and respond to pupils on the basis of widely accepted criteria of school performance. Teachers' differential expectations tend to limit educational attainment of minority and lower class students. These expectations have been learned in teacher-training school (institutions) and reflect the beliefs of the dominant societal ideology.

Some argue that the symbolic-interactionist perspective, as well as others previously discussed, tends to make either the schools or the teachers morally responsible for the existing inequality in educational opportunity (through expectations of meanings structures). As with the previous theories, this approach also overemphasizes the importance of the socioeconomic structure by suggesting that, through societal values, it imposes a particular educational ideology on teachers and schools. According to this approach, since teachers accept the dominant societal ideology, they should be held morally responsible for what goes on in schools.

To explain inequality in educational opportunity other theorists have turned to an interpretive approach that draws on Alfred Schutz's phenomenological sociology. This interpretive and phenomenological approach focuses on the social construction of knowledge and understandings of the commonsense world of everyday life, as well as the intersubjective world of common experiences, which individuals share and take for granted. The premise is that persons exist in a social world and, as social actors and actresses, they give meaning to actions and situations.The works of Alfred Schutz have also been influential in sociological theory, particularly in the areas of **phenomenology.** Schutz stressed the importance of examining the interpretive procedures or methods that individuals (including sociologists) use to arrive at the use of concepts. Thus to understand social interaction we must make explicit the obvious but "hidden" or taken-for-granted facts of interaction. Concepts such as intersubjectivity, schemes of interpretations, typifications, intentionality and taken-for-granted social knowledge were first presented by him, and will be discussed in Chapter 5.

Symbolic interactionism, and the interpretive and phenomenological perspectives provide us with a better understanding of how meanings are generated in interaction, and how the content of meanings, the relevance of intention, and the procedures and practices by which structure of meaning are made to appear real within a situation.

These orientations have been criticized for not clarifying how the leap is made from small group situations to the larger structures of organizations. For instance, if we concentrate on what definitions are important to pupils or teachers we risk overlooking the broader question of why those definitions are important. That is, we do not come to terms with the economic and political contexts within which these definitions arise. Although these theories focus on how social structure is accomplished through interaction, consideration must be given to the facts of social stratification, political control, and the social distribution of knowledge, each of which affect the practices people use to accomplish or sustain a sense of social structure or social order. Insofar as individuals function within the larger society (macro structure) they are affected by the distribution of resources and power, which then affects the interactions of individuals at the micro level, thus setting limits to the choices that they believe are available to them.

A Canadian View of Symbolic Interactionism

Several Canadian researchers have contributed to interactionist theory in the sociology of education. However, Wilfred Martin's major work, *The Negotiated Order of the School* (1976), deserves special attention. He draws on the symbolic interactionist perspective to analyze teacher-to-teacher and teacher-to-student interaction. His concern is with "interactive roles and agendas". Considering these, Martin looks at the process of negotiation, including bargaining and exchange, which occurs when the objectives of either party differ. The important point Martin makes is that this process of negotiation is truly an attempt to alter or change the way each party (individual) has defined the situation. There is much detail and rich data in Martin's book and we suggest that his work be examined carefully.

Critical Theory

Critical theory refers to both a school of thought and a process of critique. From this perspective, the claims of any critique must be questioned and must not hold to its own doctrinal assumptions. Critical theory was developed by members of the Frankfurt School, whose works were reactions to orthodox Marxism. They questioned the notion of historical inevitability and the notion that class struggle as well as the mechanisms of domination take place primarily within the confines of the labour process. They also questioned the Marxist stance of the primacy of the mode of production in shaping history. In other words, from a critical theorist's perspective, Marxism is not self-critical. Critical theorists shift the emphasis from class relations to issues of how subjectivity is constituted, and how the spheres of culture and everyday life represent a new terrain of domination. The central focus is to assess the newly emerging forms of capitalism along with the changing forms of domination and to rethink and radically reconstruct the meaning of human emancipation.

Critical theory emphasizes the following:

- social class as a unit of analysis, and everyday life as a theoretical and political sphere of investigation and struggle;
- the notion of liberation based on a variety of human needs, not just economic needs;

- a conception of society that refutes the dichotomy of subject and object and the distinction between the micro and macro levels of analysis of society;
- a rejection of economic determinism that suggests consciousness is a reflection of social being—(human behaviour is more than a reaction to capitalism); and
- social reality and subjectivity (consciousness, needs, intent, interest, motivation) possess a *dialectical* nature.

Critical theory is dialectical; that is, it recognizes that existing problems in society do not occur in isolation but are a part of the interactive process between individuals and societal structures.

> Carr and Kemmis refer to the dialectical as involving...contradictions (like the contradiction of the inadvertent oppression of less able students by a system which aspires to help all students to achieve their "full potential")...it is an open and questioning form of thinking which demands reflection back and forth between elements like, part and whole, knowledge and action, process and product, subject and object, being and becoming, rhetoric and reality or structure and function...as contradictions are revealed, new constructive thinking and...action are required to transcend the contradictory state of affairs (1983, p. 36–37).

This dialectical view permits us to see both the domination aspects and the liberation aspects of schooling. This view is contrary to the economic determinism of both conflict theorists and Neo-Marxist theorists. For example, teachers often recognize that some students are at a disadvantage in the classroom because their values and beliefs are not congruent with that of the school. They would like to change the curriculum to meet student needs, but the Ministry of Education (or its equivalent) controls the curriculum. Thus, there are opposing forces occurring at the classroom level. A dialectical analysis of such opposing social forces offers insight into objectives, activities, and practical interests of individuals in different groups. These ideas will be further elaborated in Chapter 4 when we distinguish between the theoretical perspectives and the pedagogies derived from these perspectives.

Essentially, the orientation of critical theory is derived from the recognition that experience and knowledge are both politically charged and interrelated. Thus, knowledge must be used as a practical tool for change; it must be used to transform nature and politics in a way that alleviates oppressive social conditions. For critical theorists, social phenomena are made up of dialectical forces. Briefly then, critical theorists provide insights for studying the relationship between theory and society. They have developed a dialectical framework to understand what mediates between institutions and the activities of daily life. Habermas (1968), in particular, attempted to develop a conceptual framework in which the connection between theory and practice was stressed at the level of interests which underlie the formation of knowledge itself. According to Habermas, knowledge has both a political and a practical intent. "Neutral research findings" are usually used to reinforce the status quo and to maintain the power of those in control. He argues that society is both exploitative and oppressive but also capable of being changed. His emphasis is on individual empowerment, social transformation, and the need to develop critical consciousness among students.

A Canadian Source on Critical Theory

Peter McLaren, in his book *Life in Schools* (1998), presents a critique of schooling and a detailed account of critical pedagogy based on his work in Canadian schools. His intent is to direct teachers toward a teaching process that addresses how power and empowerment are played out in the classroom. As he notes, he would like to provide teachers "with a means...to critically...face our society's complicity in the root structures of inequality" (p. 29).

In his book, McLaren includes a journal that he kept while he was teaching in a Toronto inner-city school in the 1980s. He is aware of his shifting position, from focusing on Canadian schools to U.S. schools. He argues that

> Some readers may object to my shifting context from a critique of schooling and society in the United States to an inner-city school in Canada. I would argue that the disadvantaged students of whom I speak, and the teachers who work with them, face daily struggles in the classroom that do not recognize the national boundaries between the United States and Canada (p. 33).

While the dimensions of the power structures in the United States and Canada do differ, and are no doubt played out differently in Canadian and U.S. classrooms, we would argue that the principle holds: Minorities face struggles that are linked to social structure and power.

Feminist Theory

The analysis of the relationship between women and schooling began with **liberal feminists**. The strength of their perspective was in their documentation of gender discrimination through stereotyping, bias in curricular materials, and school practices. Their aim was to change the biases and distortions in textbooks and to eliminate the sexism in practices such as different course and career counselling for girls and boys.

Although the liberal feminists' works are important, they do not situate the problems of sexism or gender differentiation in a larger sociological context. For example, liberal feminists did not look at power relations, that is, the control of the subordinate group by those in power in terms of social class and gender. Many critics of liberal feminists argued that we must place schools and schooling in the context of the social, economic, and political structures of our society.

Socialist Feminism

Feminist educational theorists interested in how structures of power and control affect the schooling process turned to **socialist feminism** to explain the relationship between women, education, and their social status position. Much of their research draws on Marxist concepts to explain differential treatment and gender inequality. For instance, Wolpe and Arnot (MacDonald) argue that **patriarchal ideology** is formed and used by the dominant class. Their works focus on the complex relationships between capitalist production, the division of labour, the family, and the educational system. These relations are all strongly influenced by patriarchal relations and ideology. (They used the term patriarchy to refer to groups of individuals or groups of organizations where males hold dominant power over females in terms of access to high status positions or privileged authority).

Wolpe analyzes, firstly, the relationship of the educational system to the state and its dominant ideological concerns, and secondly, the relationship between a sex-segregated labour force and the state. She examines in some detail the processes through which the ideology of gender is constructed through the family unit and the dominant class, and how this is mediated by the educational system. From her stance, the educational system not only functions to maintain this structure but, at the same time, is the "site of political and ideological struggle" (1978, p. 312).

However, Wolpe does not address the question of social transformations through pedagogical practice (i.e., pedagogy as the production of knowledge, identities, and values). More recently, in *Within School Walls* (1988) she argues that "to overcome the differentials operating on the basis of gender in schools, a breakdown of gender differences must occur at all levels—ideological and practical, both at home and at school" (p.199). She analyzes nonacademic (home economics and craft) and academic (mathematics, science and humanities) classes and the ideologies expressed by teachers through classroom practices. But, again, her analysis remains at the structural level, focusing on societal ideologies. She writes,

> the practice associated with the integration of subjects for boys and girls appears restricted by a set of ideologies which relate specifically to gender identities in terms of home-centered activities. In other words, it is quite legitimate to integrate all courses provided this does not represent any threat to the status quo of the gender-based division of labour both in the home and place of work (p. 224).

MacDonald (Arnot)(1980) also argues that to more clearly understand women's positions in capitalist society we must reassess existing explanations of schooling which have not focused on the "sexual division of labor within the school and its impact in determining the relations between the family, schooling and labor processes" (p.13). She discusses two major theories within the sociology of education, the theory of social reproduction (Althusser, 1971; Bowles and Gintis, 1976) and the theory of cultural reproduction of class structure (Bernstein, 1973). Her objective is to use these theories "as the basis for an explanatory model of the forms of women's education within societies which are both capitalist and patriarchal" (p.13).

In particular, she uses Bernstein's (1980) argument that forms of social organization are reproduced by the school through the "categorization of pupils by age, sex and social class" (p.22) and are reinforced through the classification of knowledge, teacher-student relations, the school structure, and forms of evaluation. An analysis of these factors reveals the operation of gender codes operating to direct males and females towards the acquisition of particular forms of symbolic property such as ideas, attitudes, and certificates and degrees (p.13).

For MacDonald, it is the specific aspects of patriarchal ideology—sexual power relations and gender categorization—which must be researched and explained in a sociological theory of women's education. She accepts the theories of the class structure but argues that these must be modified to include gender differentiation within both schooling and the capitalist work structure.

More recently, Arnot (nee MacDonald) maintains her argument that there is a material base to patriarchy and a class structure to gender differentiation, and has changed the concept of "reproduction" in favor of the concept of **male hegemony**. Here we use Gramsci's (1971) concept of hegemony. He refers to hegemony as a world view(s) or power structures which are maintained by the dominant class. This power goes unquestioned, as natural and commonsense, by those who are subordinated. It refers to a whole range of structures and activities, as well as values, attitudes, beliefs, and morality that in various ways support the established order, including class and male interests (1994, p. 85–6).

By introducing the concept of male hegemony to analyze class and gender, Arnot hopes to develop a theory of gender classification that is class-based and would "expose the structural and interactional features of gender reproduction and conflict in families, in schools, and in workplaces" (p. 97). Also, in continuing to believe that Bernstein's theory of classification systems is useful to developing a theory of gender codes that is class-based, she states:

> The idea of gender codes relates well to the concept of hegemony; both refer to the social organization of family and school life where definitions of feminine and masculine are taught in such a way as to accept the natural hierarchy of male over female—the superiority of men in society (p.97).

For Arnot, the important aspects of any theory of gender are that

- gender categories are arbitrary social constructs carried out by social institutions (schools, churches, mass media);
- gender classifications are not universal or static;
- gender categories are constructed through a concept of gender differences" (p.101); and
- educational differences are essentially secured via the family, educational system, and structural division of labour.

Arnot's position does not truly shift from her original position, which is framed by social and cultural reproduction theories. She argues that Marxist feminist accounts of the schooling process do not explain how patriarchal oppression has its own dynamics and concerns in gender struggles because of their main focus on Marxist class categories (1994, p.93). However, the concept of male hegemony does not account for how patriarchal ideology is sustained through educational practice. That is, she speaks to a Marxist perspective to provide teachers with practical classroom strategies which would demystify the illusion of equal educational opportunity, and to explicitly address the hierarchical structure and political power that is found within schools.

The Marxist feminist focus on patriarchal ideology, which undergirds the economic and political relations that characterize the educational system, leads to fundamental misconceptions about the centrality of subjectivity in the concept of patriarchal ideology. There is also the problem that the analyses provided by Wolpe and Arnot do not provide productive insights into feminist's power relations with either men or women. An understanding of how feminists themselves use power and knowledge to explain subordination is required. This lack of clarification of feminists' use of knowledge and power has serious implications for theorists and pedagogists whose aim is to transform educational practices.

Some feminist educational theorists are presently challenging existing Marxist feminist theory framed by class and class reproduction. The specific interest in these writings is on the oppressive nature of male discourse. That is, knowledge that is controlled by patriarchy ensures the perpetuation of domination.

Diamond and Quinby (1988) note how Foucault's work influenced many feminists' analyses. Foucault analyzed modern discourses on power. His primary concerns were with the history of scientific thought, the development of technologies of power and domination, and the arbitrariness of modern social institutions. For feminists, his analysis of power offers a way in which class, race, and gender differences can be taken into account. Both Foucault and the feminists identify the body as the site of power, that is, the locus of domination through which docility is accomplished and subjectivity constituted. They focus on the role of discourse in producing and sustaining hegemonic power. Both criticize western masculine elite as it produces or proclaims universal truths about freedom and human nature.

Discourse is a central concept in Foucault's analytical framework. We use the concept of discourses or **discursive practices**, as Gore(1992) does, to refer to what can be said and thought, and to who can speak when and with what authority. Gore also looks at discursive practices to highlight the ways in which language, subjectivity, social institutions, intellectuals and power are related (Gore, 1993, p. 159). For a sample of interpretations of Foucault's definition of discourse see Lather, 1991; and Luke and Gore, 1992.

Postmodernist Feminism

Some writings show a development of feminist educational theory which critiques not only the liberal feminist and socialist feminist perspectives, but also the critical educational theory. This literature represents a **postmodernist** analysis grounded in the work of Foucault.

Postmodernist theory addresses the relationship between power and knowledge, the negative effects of master narratives, and the way institutions are not only controlling but are controlled. In the broadest sense, postmodernism challenges the idea of universal truths or what some refer to as master narratives. It is a critique of the dominant forms of analysis or accepted truths (e.g., Marxism, early tradition of critical theory).

Although many postmodernist feminists draw on Foucault's works, they question his lack of focus on political struggle, and the danger of being thwarted by an elitist but academically respectable perspective that ignores gender issues, as well as his lack of an analysis of women's experience of men's power, which is a form of domination backed by the dominant group. For Foucault, the relation of power to knowledge is inseparable. His notions of power-knowledge challenge assumptions that ideology can be demystified and that undistorted truth can be attained. Power is everywhere and available to all at some level. Therefore, systematic subordination of women by women as well as systematic domination of women by men are no longer seen as categories of power relations. Moreover, Foucault does not help us distinguish between the kinds of differences which cut across women's lives.

Postmodern feminists argue that we must be able to identify the structural contradictions of these differences, which cannot be captured in terms of discursive analysis. It matters who is speaking. Weiler and Mitchell (1992, p. 5) state that postmodernist theory can be seen as a perspective which challenges universal truths. That is, in the broadest sense it challenges the idea of universal truths or what some refer to as *master narratives*. It is a critique of the dominant forms of analysis or accepted truths (for example, Marxism and the early tradition of critical theory) that concerns itself with mediation of language in human thought and action. It recognizes the function of discourse in constructing identities and subject positions. The point is to reveal the structuring of one's own discourse (the way we talk and write) in existing disciplines and to bring the reader into the inquiry as an analytic partner in deconstructing and destabilizing theories or texts. This approach contributes to the process of demystification and social change.

Essentially, feminists drawing on postmodern theory call into question the privileged position of white male theorists. They challenge the critical educational theorists, who are predominantly male, to examine how their assumptions and thoughts affect their discursive practices.

Some Canadian Sources on Feminist Theory

Gaskell, McLaren and Novogrodsky, in *Claiming an Education* (1989), provide us with evidence of women's disadvantage in education in Canada. Among the important issues they discuss are the problems of inequality in educational opportunity and how women have participated in and achieved in the educational system. Dorothy Smith (1987), in *The Everyday World as Problematic*, focuses on various aspects of women's situations in education and societal relations, and she provides us with research strategies to develop a sociology for women. Marlene Mackie (1987, 1994) gives an excellent account of gender socialization and gender relations in Canada. Other important case studies have been carried out by Gaskell, McLaren and Novogradsky (1989), and Gaskell (1992).

SUMMARY/CONCLUSIONS

This chapter began with an introduction to the origins of sociology of education. We then presented the major theories—functionalist, conflict/Neo-Marxist, critical, and feminist—which sociologists use to explain the relationship between schooling and society.

In the 1950s the concern was for the ways in which the education system related to both divisions of labor and social stratification (the ranking of the individuals on the basis of education, occupation, and income). The major theoretical perspective used to analyze the relationship between schools and society was referred to as functionalism. Functionalists saw education in terms of its function to provide a literate and adaptable workforce to meet the needs of an advanced technological society. That is, the education system functions in the interest of society. Functionalists were concerned with reforms that would lead to a stable social order rather than addressing the problem of social inequality. The functionalists emphasized meritocracy. Meritocracy assumes that each individual has a unique set of abilities, and it is their individual effort and abilities that will help them succeed in school. Thus, according to this view, the number of years spent in school predicts occupational achievement and, therefore, social status.

In the 1960s, sociologists began to argue that there was a great deal of wastage of working-class ability due to streaming and tracking in schools. The extent of inequality in education was documented, but the causes of inequality remained unexplained. In the late 1960s and 1970s, a group of sociologists referred to as conflict, Neo-Marxist, or radical theorists focused on the relationship between political and economic forces and the education system. The education system was viewed as reproducing the class structure of modern industrialist society and functioning in the interest of the dominant group. For example, the belief was that education is used to control the patterns of thought, sentiment, and behaviour of the working class. Essentially, education was thought of as authority and social control. The differences between conflict theorists lay not so much in the level of their analyses as in what they considered the implications for social change. Conflict theorists argued that if the education system was to play a part in change, then pupils and teachers would need to be radicalized to play a part in the class struggle.

The symbolic-interaction, interpretive, and phenomonological theorists focused on classroom dynamics and curricular issues. This approach was antifunctional and antideterministic. The central task became an examination of the participants in the educational process through an exploration of their perceptions and assumptions as well as their interactions with each other. There was a change in method, most significantly, in the exchange of observation for the social survey, and a change in what were considered to be the important problem areas that should be studied. The questions which interested this new generation of researchers were no longer which children fail, or even why they fail, but what was the nature or status of school knowledge, or the nature of failure itself.

Attention turned to the assumptions held within the school, especially by teachers, on the meaning of success and failure, on definitions of good and bad pupils, and on differences between what teachers said and what they did. Thus, the concept of education as culture became important. The management of knowledge became a key issue. It is not how we sort and select people on the basis of individual effort and ability that is important, rather it is how the curriculum is selected and legitimated.

Sociologists critiqued the above approaches, and, in the mid-80s and the 90s, critical-feminist and antiracist pedagogies emerged. Critical theory emerged because some researchers found it unacceptable to only focus on capitalist relations of production and their relations to education—that is, the social and cultural reproduction model was rejected. Thus, theoretical critique and discourse analysis has become the primary focus, and much of the current research aims at curriculum transformation and the empowerment of teachers and students.

Gender dimensions have also become a concern in educational research. Feminist researchers look at domination and exclusion in the classroom, as well as subjectivity and identity. While research relating to how class and gender inequalities are reproduced in school cultures is fruitful, research on racial inequality in this context has not been as productive. Antiracist research focuses on the ways that curricula and school practices reflect structural realities that devalue the self-image, culture, and identity of visible minority students.

The main differences between the above approaches are their implications for social change. It is important to assess the implications and consequences of the different theoretical perspectives and what each considers to be the solution to educational problems.

The intent of this chapter has been to introduce the major theories in the field of sociology of education. While the contributions of Canadian sociologists have not been numerous, they are important because of what they illuminate—the differences in educational practice in Canada, the United States or Britain, for example. There is much more to each author's work(s) than that which is presented here. Interested students can note the suggested readings at the end of this chapter.

KEY TERMS

correspondence principle or theory	interpretive sociology	self
critical theory	liberal feminism	socialist feminism
cultural capital	male hegemony	status culture
definition of the situation	me	status groups
discursive practices	Neo-Marxis theory	structures of dominance
ideal types	patriarchal ideology	symbolic interaction
interpretive procedures	phenomenology	
	postmodernist feminism	

DISCUSSION QUESTIONS

1. Discuss the primary focus of and the differences between each sociological theory presented in this chapter.

2. What, if any, problems do you see with each theory as they relate to the process of schooling?

3. To what extent do you agree with any of the theories? Explain why.

RECOMMENDED READINGS/REFERENCES

Althusser, L. (1971) Ideology and ideological state apparatuses. In *Lenin and Philosophy and Other Essays.* (B. Brewster, Trans.) (pp. 127–193). London: New Left Books.

Arnot, M. (1994). Male hegemony, social class, and women's education. In L. Stone (Ed.), *The education feminist reader* (pp. 84–104). New York: Routledge.

Aronowitz, S., & Giroux, H. (Eds.). (1993). *Still under siege.* Connecticut: Bergin and Garvey.

Bélanger, P. W., & Rocher, G. (Eds.) (1975). *Ecole et societé au Quebec.* Montreal: Hurtubise HMH.

Bernstein, B. (1973). *Call codes and control*. London: Routledge Kegan Paul Ltd.

Bourdieu, P., & Passeron, J. C. (1977). *Reproduction in education: Society and culture*. California: Sage.

Bourdieu, P. (1986). The forms of capital. In I. C. Richardson (Ed.), *Handbook of theory and research for the sociology of education*. (R. Nice, Trans.) (pp. 241–258). New York: Greenwood Press.

Bowles, S., & Gintis, H. (1976). *Schooling in capitalist America*. New York: Basic Books.

Carr, W. & Kemmis, S (1983). *Becoming critical: Knowing through action research*. Victoria: Dean University

Clement, W. (1975). *The Canadian corporate elite: An analysis of economic power*. Toronto: McClelland & Stewart.

Coleman, J. (1968). The concept of equality of opportunity. *Harvard Educational Review, 38*, 7–32.

Collins, R. (1977). Functional and conflict theories of educational stratification. *American Sociological Review, 36* (6), 1002–19.

Cooley, C. H. (1956). *Human nature and the social order*. Glencoe, Ill.: Free Press.

Diamond, I., & Quinby, L. (Eds.). (1988). *Feminisms and Foucault: Reflections on resistance*. Boston: Northwestern University Press.

Dreeben, R. (1968). *On what is learned in school*. Reading Mass.: Addison–Wesley.

Durkheim, E. (1956). *Education and society*. Glencoe, Il.: The Free Press.

Freire, P. (1968). *Pedagogy of the oppressed*. New York: Seabury Press.

Gaskell, J. (1992). *Gender matters from school to work*. Toronto: OISE Press.

Gaskell, J., McLaren, A., & Novogrodsky, H. (1989). *Claiming and education: Feminism and Canadian schools*. Toronto: Education Foundation.

Giroux, H. (1992). *Border crossings*. New York: Routledge.

Gore, J. (1992). Feminist politics in radical pedagogy, In C. Luke & J. Gore (Eds.), *Feminisims and critical pedagogies* (pp. 25–53). New York: Routledge.

Gore, J. (1993). *The struggle for pedagogies*. New York: Routledge.

Gramsci, A. (1971). *Selections from the prison notebooks*. (Ed. and trans.) Q. Hoare & G. Nowell-Smith. New York: International Publishers.

Habermas, J. (1968). *Knowledge and human interests*. Boston: Beacon Press

Lather, P. (1992). Post-critical pedagogies: A feminist reading. In C. Luke & J. Gore, *Feminisms and critical pedagogies* (pp. 120–137). New York Routledge.

Livingstone, D.W. (1983). *Class, ideologies and educational futures*. London: Routledge.

Livingstone, D. W. (1985). *Social crisis and school*. Toronto: Garamond Press.

Livingstone, D. W. (1994). Searching for missing links: Neo–Marxist theories of education. In L. Irwin, & D. MacLennan (Eds.), *Sociology of education in Canada: Critical perspectives in theory, research and practice.(pp.* 55–82). Toronto: Copp Clark Longman:.

Luke, C. & Gore, J. (1992). *Feminisims and critical pedagogies*. New York: Routledge.

MacDonald, M. (1980). Socio–cultural reproduction and women's education. In R. Deem. (Ed.), *Schooling for women's work* (pp. 13–25). Boston: Routledge and Kegan Paul Ltd.

Mackie, M. (1987). *Constructing women and men.* Toronto: Holt, Rinehardt & Winston.

Mackie, M. (1994). Socialization. In R. Hagedorn (Ed.), *Sociology* (5th. ed.) (pp. 89–120). Toronto: Harcourt Brace and Company.

Martell, G. (Ed.). (1974). *The politics of the Canadian public school.* Toronto: James Lorimer and Company.

Martin, W. (1976). *The negotiated order of the school.* Toronto: MacMillan.

McLaren, P. (1995) *Critical Pedagogy and Predatory Culture.* New York: Routledge.

McLaren, P. (1998). *Life in schools: An introduction to critical pedagogy in the foundations of education (3rd ed.).* Don Mills: Langerman.

Mead, G. H. (1934). *Mind, self and society.* Chicago: University of Chicago Press.

Mifflen, F., & Mifflen, S. (1982). *The sociology of education.* Calgary: Detselig Enterprise Ltd.

Murphy, R. (1979). *Sociological theories of education.* Toronto: McGraw–Hill Ryerson.

Nelsen, R.,& Nock, D. (Eds.). (1978). *Reading, writing and riches: Education and the socio–economic order in North America.* Kitchener: Between the Lines.

Parsons, T. (1959). The school class as a social system: Some of its functions in American society. *Harvard Educational Review*, 29, (pp. 647–665).

Persell, C. H. (1977). *Education and inequality.* New York: The Free Press.

Porter, J. (1965). *The vertical mosaic: An analysis of social class and power in Canada.* Toronto: University of Toronto Press.

Schutz, A. (1973). *Collected papers: The problem of social reality.* The Hague: Martinus Nijhoff.

Simon, R. (1987, April). Empowerment as a pedagogy of possibility. *Language Arts, 64* (4) pp. 370–382.

Smith, D. (1987). *The everyday world as problematic: A feminist sociology.* Toronto: Univeristy of Toronto Press.

Weber, M. (1947). *The theory of social and economic organization.* New York: The Free Press.

Weiler, K. (1988). *Women teaching for change: Gender, class and power.* Massachusetts: Garvey Publishers.

Weiler, K. (1991). Freire and a feminist pedagogy of difference. *Harvard Educational Review, 16* (4) pp. 449–474.

Weiler, K., & Mitchell, C. (Eds.), (1992). *What schools can do: Critical pedagogy and practice.* New York: State University of New York.

Wolpe, A.M. (1978). Education and the sexual division of labour. In A. Kuhn, & A.M. Wolpe, (Eds.). *Feminism and Materialism* (pp. 290–328). Boston: Routledge and Kegan Paul Ltd.

Wolpe, A.M. (1988). *Within school walls*. New York: Routledge.

Wotherspoon, T. (Ed.). (1987). *The political economy of Canadian schooling*. Toronto: Methuen.

Wotherspoon, T. (1998). *The sociology of education in Canada: Critical Perspectives*. Toronto: Oxford University Press.

Chapter

3

THE ORGANIZATION OF TEACHING AND LEARNING

Chapter Objectives

In this chapter we look at the organization of teaching and learning. The purpose is to show how societal, school, and personal variables interact to affect the life of teachers and learners within schools. The chapter begins with a discussion of schools as formal organizations, then moves on to informal relations within schools and to the norms of the teaching profession. This will be followed by a discussion of models of teacher education and models of teaching. The chapter will end with a section on curriculum. Wherever relevant we use the theoretical perspectives from Chapter 2 to illuminate the likely effects of the organization of teaching and learning on achievement and on the perpetuation of social inequality.

THE SCHOOL AS A FORMAL ORGANIZATION

A **formal organization** is a type of group or interaction system whose behaviour is directed towards specific goals. Unlike family groups, where relations are informal and variable, a formal organization is just that, formalized. It is characterized by a complex division of labour, clearly defined job roles and relationships, hierarchically ranked subdivisions and positions, and large size. A formal organization exists regardless of the particular individuals who work within it, that is, any individual can be replaced. This implies that formal organizations have established structures with entrenched obligations, rights, privileges, and procedures that its participants agree to and abide by contractually.

Schools are formal organizations, and like most formal organizations they are also bureaucracies. A **bureaucracy** is characterized by rationality and efficiency in the performance of complex tasks towards the attainment of specific goals (Blau & Scott, 1962; Gordon, 1975; Spencer, 1979).

The expected behaviours of individuals who occupy positions in a formal organization are contained within formal job descriptions and also governed by shared ideas regarding what constitutes appropriate behaviour. These ideas are called **norms**. Norms may be explicit, as in the case of rules for carrying out particular tasks, or they may be implicit, as in the "rules" governing interaction between people occupying different positions within the hierarchy, or between people who belong to different social classes, races, languages or ethnic groups. Thus, we see the likelihood that every formal organization is inclined to develop a parallel **informal organization** or interaction system. Patterns of informal relations are based on social differences—personal attributes such as race or position within the organization (formal status).

Formal divisions within the organization, between which there may be competition, such as school departments for instance, are a source of subgroups that may contribute further to the informal system of interaction. Informal relations within an organization may or may not be functional as far as they affect the attainment of the organization's goals.

Schools have long been regarded as formal organizations, but there are indications that the organization of schooling may be in a state of transition, reflecting society's change from an industrial to a high-tech form of production. For the moment, however, we will proceed with the discussion of the school as a formal organization, since the changes that are in progress cannot be understood if we are not fully aware of the way things have been.

One of the Canadian educational sociologists who explored the influence of the school's formal organization on the informal organization is W. B. W. Martin (1975; 1976). He found that a number of factors—grade level taught, subject taught, gender, age, and years of teaching experience—contribute to the informal lines of communication among teachers in schools. Where there is more than one class per grade and where grades form the major structural division within a school teachers of the same grade tend to form subgroups based on their commonly shared experiences and problems with children of the same age.

Martin also compared regularly organized schools with **open-structured schools** where differences in the normative expectations governing teachers were found. In open-structured schools, where children are grouped according to achievement level or interest, rather than simply by age and grade, teachers work in teams of two or more. Thus, students, space, and materials are shared. Members of the same teaching team must cooperate and agree on the specific instructional goals of their subgroup.

Martin found that teachers felt a primary loyalty to their team (subgroup) rather than to the larger teacher group. In contrast, in regularly organized schools, where teachers work in isolation from each other, the entire teacher group is comparable to a single team in which general agreement over program goals is expected. Disagreements threaten the cohesion of the group.

The foregoing is important to our understanding of alternatively organized schools, such as those that contain different learning streams or tracks. A familiar example in Canada would be schools that contain both a French-immersion stream and a regular English-taught stream. In these schools the streams do not share the same program objectives: one stream is concerned with bilingual education, the other possesses the goals of a regular English school. The immersion-stream and the English-stream teachers each constitute de-facto teaching teams that cut across grade level horizontally. English-stream and immersion-stream teachers of the same grade level do not share the same objectives, nor do they share the same problems with learners. Both streams, however, are normally under the direction of one principal and arc subject to the same curriculum guidelines.

Thus on the one hand the teacher group is subject to the regular norms of the teaching profession, while on the other hand their roles as teachers are defined by their membership in the two major linguistic groups—French speaking and English speaking—that make up the larger society. This sets the stage for teachers to occupy conflicting roles and for this conflict to further influence their interactions towards each other. As Cleghorn and Genesee reported (1984), these informal interaction features of school organization are observable to learners, contributing to the role that schools play in perpetuating the long-standing perceptions that members of each group hold towards each other.

The Teaching Profession, Teachers' Roles, and Teacher Groups

Teaching is a unique profession in many ways (Levin & Young, 1994). First of all there is debate as to whether or not teaching is a full profession, since the responsibilities, rights, and duties of a teacher are not fully comparable to those of, say, a lawyer or a dentist. While the teacher is obliged to teach children to the best of his or her ability, the teacher is not legally responsible for the results; despite an increasing tendency to make teachers and schools accountable, success or failure to learn "belongs" to the child.

Second, the teacher-student client relationship is not direct; teachers do not bill students directly for their services but rather are paid by the education authorities—the government, the school board, the community—or, in private schools, by the school from tuition paid by parents.

Third, unlike doctors or lawyers, teachers possess a great deal of personal knowledge about their chosen profession from their own past experience as learners, prior to embarking on a teaching-education program. That is, before being educated as teachers, most teachers, if not all, hold distinct images of what constitutes either a good teacher or a poor teacher (Weber & Mitchell, 1995). It is upon this extensive base of prior knowledge that teachers are socialized into the profession, or quasi-profession (Dickinson, 1995; Goodlad, 1990).

Although teachers are socialized somewhat differently for teaching the elementary and secondary grades, some generalizations can be made. The norms of the teaching profession emphasize the importance of close working relationships and feelings of group cohesion, despite the fact that teachers usually work in isolation from their colleagues and their rewards are classroom centred. Teachers are further governed by norms of harmony and cooperation. They are expected to share common perspectives with regard to program objectives and to present a united front to the outside world, including the world of parents. They are expected to share ideas, supplies, and chores. The allocation of time is an important issue among teachers. Their day is marked by frequent reminders of time, and spare time, in particular, is to be shared equally. Discussions in teacher groups tend to focus on students, taking the form of anecdotal accounts of classroom events. Controversial issues tend to be avoided (Jackson, 1968; Lortie, 1975).

Friendship patterns among teachers are likely to be based on personal attributes such as age or sex, or, as indicated earlier, to stem from membership in the same formal subgroups, such as grade level taught, teaching stream, subject taught or departmental affiliation (Greenberger & Sorensen, 1970). Older teachers normally enjoy considerable status among their colleagues; their opinions and advice are sought by younger teachers. In the case of immersion schools cited above (Cleghorn & Genesee, 1984), the older teachers were affiliated with the English stream and the younger teachers with the more recently implemented immersion stream, thus the advice of the older teachers was perceived as irrelevant to the needs of the younger teachers. This division, among other factors, seriously influenced the otherwise expected harmony of the teacher group. Thus we can say that factors such as gender, language, race, or ethnicity may provide sources of conflict among teachers and interfere with the sense of group collegiality.

As we saw earlier, in multilingual, multicultural, and multiracial communities, relations between members of the different groups may be reflected in their interaction patterns. In schools, interaction patterns occur both among and between teachers and learners. Such patterns contribute to the socialization of children to the norms governing the interactions between members of the same groups in society at large. Thus, the manner in which conflict among teachers is managed within such schools is clearly important, not only for the functioning of the school towards its sometimes varied goals, but also for the attitudinal climate the students are exposed to.

Knowing that teacher groups place considerable importance on harmony, it is not surprising then that several researchers have found that teachers use a number of interaction strategies to prevent conflict from coming to a head and to recreate an appearance of collegiality when disagreements or inter-group tensions arise. These strategies include bargaining, persuasion, negotiation, impression management, ingratiation, insincere expression of affect, and denial that a problem exists (Corwin, 1965; Martin, 1975).

As we will see, the norms of the teaching profession contribute to the culture of the profession, laying the basis for considerable resistance to social change. When individual teachers try to take it upon themselves to implement change within the classroom, or even within the general interaction patterns of the teacher group, there is bound to be a reaction from other teachers, from parents, or from the school administration. Some of the examples that come to mind include a female science teacher, known to the authors, whose goal is to see "black girls enter the sciences." This teacher reports that her greatest struggle is to get other teachers to take her seriously.

Another teacher reported to us that some parents become nearly abusive towards them when faced with math homework that they themselves cannot understand; they want their children to memorize multiplication tables (yet parents are against authoritarianism). And a French-speaking teacher working in an early French-immersion school was ostracized by the other French- and English-speaking teachers when she suggested that the day after New Years' Day should be a holiday for French Canadian teachers who often have to travel far from traditional family festivities to get back to work in time.

It is of note that teacher associations mainly deal with financial and contractual considerations, rarely with ideological or philosophical issues in education. Yet it is within such organizations that there may be some hope for teachers' voices to be heard; certainly at the level of the school the individual teacher risks a lot by openly questioning the status quo or by acting to bring about change on her or his own.

The Role of the Principal

The foregoing brings us to the topic of the school principal. A complex set of norms govern the role of the principal. In a school that is organized into teaching teams, the principal's role is more diffuse than in regular schools. In the former, the principal becomes the manager of and the link between the different teams, while also playing a pivotal role in the management of conflict (Lortie, 1975).

The principal plays a key role in the decision-making process and influences the relationship between teachers and the world outside the classroom. Although teachers normally enjoy a high degree of privacy and autonomy in the classroom, as stated earlier, the classroom, the students, and the supplies belong to others (the school board and parents). A teacher's autonomy is limited by the principal's authority to enter the classroom at any time; if the principal is perceived as offering help to the teacher their autonomy may be willingly relinquished.

Teachers look to the principal to deal with difficult students and parents as well as with teachers who fail to do their share of the school's chores. However, Martin and Macdonell (1978) and Lortie (1975) found that when a principal behaves in an authoritarian manner towards teachers, resistance towards the principal then serves to unify the teacher group. On the other hand, if the principal by-passes a teacher to deal directly with a child's poor academic performance or with unacceptable behaviour, the problem is linked to the child rather than to poor teaching. It is by these means that the principal can help teachers. It is also through such mechanisms that the status of the teaching profession remains quasi-professional.

Teachers differ in the amount they want to be involved in the decision-making process, but they are similar in that they all want to be consulted. In schools with large staff groups, the principal will meet regularly with representatives of the entire staff. The primary function of this group is to provide the principal with a way of exerting authority in accordance with democratic norms. In staff meetings the principal's wishes are made known, negotiation takes place, agreement is reached, and the rest of the staff is then consulted about the decision.

The principal is also expected to protect teachers and to act as a buffer between them and the outside world—parents, school board demands, even the effects of social and technological change. In return for such protection the principal receives support and respect from the teachers.

TEACHER EDUCATION: SOME CANADIAN TRENDS

In this section we look at a few of the current models that are found for educating teachers in Canada. Where it is instructive, we will draw on comparisons with other parts of the world. In line with the general view of this book, we will see that the ways Canada educates its teachers reflect a number of on-going debates in education, as well as prevailing attitudes about how learning occurs and the ways that children, in particular, should be treated in school. Thus, this section will be followed by a brief discussion of models of teaching so that the reader may consider the extent to which the approaches that are advocated for use in the classroom agree with the ways teachers are prepared to teach.

The teaching profession and teacher education in Canada have changed dramatically over the last forty years, as is the case elsewhere. For example, in 1960 a high school graduate (usually a woman) who wished to teach elementary school went directly to a teachers' college, which was usually affiliated with a university. If she wanted to teach the lower primary grades, she spent one year at the college; if she wanted to teach the upper primary grades, she spent two years. Forty years later, as the year 2000 approaches, a primary school teacher must first obtain a bachelor degree in education (in some provinces); alternatively, she must hold a bachelor degree in arts or science, followed by a year or two of teacher education in a university setting. This pattern of spiraling qualifications required to become a school teacher has also occurred in other parts of the world.

Is There a Crisis in Teacher Education?

The word *crisis* appears often both in newspaper reports of education and in people's conversations about education. We hear about the crisis of falling standards, the crisis in discipline, the crisis of violence in the schools. And we hear about the literacy crisis. A crisis is a situation in flux where people do not know which way to turn. A situation is not a crisis if people know what to do. In this section we will take a brief look at the supposed crisis in teacher education. Later in the chapter we will turn to the notion of a literacy crisis. In each case we would argue that the crisis is not where people commonly think it is, but it may be true that they do not know where to turn.

Teachers get blamed for many things. Terms like "back to basics," "accountability," "teacher quality," and "falling standards" come easily into discussions about teaching. When various reforms and innovations in education fail to produce the desired results, teachers tend to be blamed, people forgetting that most changes in classrooms are not decided on by teachers or other educators but by politically motivated officers within a Ministry of Education. Teachers rarely have much say in what they are to teach, though once they are in the classroom they enjoy a high degree of autonomy in deciding how they will actually cover the curriculum.

In some parts of the world reports of a crisis in teacher education are accepted without question and proposals for reform are put forth as possible solutions. In actuality, the problems in education are not well defined, in part because they are not adequately researched. The problems are so multifaceted that single solutions are inadequate. Nevertheless, Canada, from time to time, joins what is in effect an international discussion, with questions centering on such issues as the length of training, the location of training, and the content of training. Additional questions surround the issue of theory versus practice, with England leading the way in discrediting the usefulness of theory, and Germany and France, in contrast, requiring a total of four or five years of undergraduate study of subject and theory prior to two years of practice before certification (Tulasiewicz, 1996).

In Canada, Grimmett and Wideen (1995) build on the earlier work of Schön (1983) to make a case for a novel mix of school- and university-based teacher education. They suggest that early, extensive, and well-directed exposure to teaching practice coupled with time for theoretical input and reflection within an undergraduate program may succeed in effectively linking theory and practice, helping teachers to know why they use particular teaching strategies and to be able to account for their use.

Debates in Teacher Education

There are two main areas of debate in teacher education and these debates influence how we think about teaching. The first has to do with the question of what it is that teachers need to know: do they need to know thoroughly the subject matter that they teach, do they need to know a set of methods for teaching, or do they need to know about the learning styles and abilities of the learners? Obviously teachers need to know all of these things; however, the emphasis in most teacher education courses has been on either one or the other.

The second area of debate relates to the locale and timing of training: should teachers be fully prepared to teach before they enter the classroom (pre-service) or should the majority of training be provided over the course of the teaching career (in-service)? While the tendency has been to pre-service training, there are pressures to increase the amount of in-service teacher education, due to the fact that teachers' knowledge of a subject is quickly surpassed by new knowledge, driven both by technological developments and by new ways of thinking about learning.

The tendency in Canada is for most teacher education to take place prior to hiring, however, this model is not suitable for all parts of the world. For example, in many still-developing countries the school systems have expanded in the last fifteen to twenty years more rapidly than the number of trained and qualified teachers.Thus, untrained or undertrained teachers are hired and then provided with a series of in-service courses, sometimes through distance education, eventually obtaining the necessary formal qualifications and certification. Although it may not be ideal to have children taught by inexperienced and undertrained teachers, there is some evidence to suggest that on-the-job teacher training may be as or more effective than pre-service training, when pre-service training involves little classroom practice. This is because practicing teachers can bring immediate situations and problems to the courses they take and then try out what they learn in their classrooms. In this way, as suggested earlier, the gap between theory, as presented in lectures by teacher educators, and practice in the classroom may be narrowed.

One of the most difficult aspects of organizing education for teachers is in fitting their education to the kind of situation that they are most likely to encounter. For example, how often are teachers truly prepared for the inclusive classroom where learning disabled and physically disabled children are grouped with students who do not have such difficulties? What preparation do teachers have in some of the still-developing countries for mixed-grade classes numbering 80 or more pupils (and no paper, chalk or textbooks)? (Tabulawa, 1998). Where are teachers helped to think creatively about the situations they will find themselves in? Where are they given the autonomy to be true professionals, free to implement the creative solutions that they themselves devise? Finally, how can teachers prepare themselves to teach in settings where they are "the other"? We will explain what we mean by this in the following section where we examine the use of teacher narratives as a device for generating reflection, and ultimately, reform in the teacher-education process. As a model for educating teachers, the use of narratives has arisen both from critical pedagogy and feminist pedagogy, topics that will be elaborated on more fully in Chapter 4.

According to Laird (1988) there is a need to reconceptualize the teaching profession because it has long been perceived as a "women's profession" while at the same time it has not been taken seriously as a profession. Laird notes the supposedly gender-neutral advice of many task forces on teaching that consistently call for reforms that translate into social action while ignoring the contributions of feminist scholars such as Shrewsbury (1987), Martin (1985), Rich (1985) and the Holmes Group (1986). According to these theorists, feminist pedagogy alters the basic structure of the entire taken-for-granted patriarchal paradigm of schooling (Laird, p.452); it is interactive and seeks for women to write their own truths. It suggests that "a community of learners ... act responsibly toward one another and the subject matter and ... apply that learning to social action"(p. 450).

Acker (1988) notes, however, how seldom it is that teachers act decisively to bring about change and how the norms of the teaching profession which promote harmony in teacher groups have been so internalized as to insure that the inclination to resist does not surface. Acker argues that teachers are caught up in gender regimes:

> the pattern of practices that constructs various kinds of masculinity and femininity among staff and students, orders them in terms of prestige and power, and constructs a sexual division of labor within the institution...gender is a major organizing principle.... (pp. 309–310).

Gender regimes carry teachers along "unwittingly in their wake" (Acker, 1988, p. 310). For teachers, to resist is to disrupt; to disrupt is to violate the norms of the teaching profession. Instead, sex biases in the classroom may be seen in terms of "natural" differences; social class biases are understood in terms of the importance of remediating **cultural deficits**, and the focus on the individual child in child-centred classrooms provides a neutral, ideological side-stepping of racial, ethnic, religious, and sex differences in the classroom (Flores, Cousin & Diaz, 1991).

Teacher Narratives in Teacher Education

Nowadays teachers may be educated in a relatively monocultural environment but later find themselves teaching in a highly multicultural school setting. Alternatively, a teacher may choose to teach abroad or in a religious/ethnic private school setting within a multicultural society. In either case, a teacher may be ill prepared for (sometimes vast) cultural differences between their expectations and their students' expectations. The teacher then finds herself in the position of "other." That is, the teacher may well be a member of the society's so-called dominant group, but, by virtue of her gender, race, culture, language or religion, is a minority in the school setting where she has accepted a teaching position.

As Baverstock-Angelus (1999) reports, this could be a white Canadian teacher in an Inuit school in the Arctic, a Christian teacher in a Muslim school, a Canadian teacher in a Korean school, or an anglophone in a French school. When teachers who have taught under such circumstances share their stories, it becomes evident how useful narratives can be for developing a shared consciousness, an understanding of what it feels like for students who are "other" and what intercultural communication really means.

Teacher **narratives** are stories that tell of lived experiences, struggles, self-reflections, personal growth, and empowerment. They tell of the development of cross-cultural understanding and the shedding of preconceived ideas. The following are excerpts from two teachers' narratives, the first from a Christian teacher in an Islamic school for girls in Montreal, the second from a non-native teacher in a Cree school in Northern Quebec. In each case, the teachers move from feelings of isolation and powerlessness (even oppression) to new understandings and a personal sense of strength. In addition, situations that were openly conflictual brought reflection and an understanding of both sides of an issue.

Teaching in an Islamic School

For the job interview I donned a long-sleeved dress that fell below my knees. I was greeted by two ladies wearing hijabs (a scarf that covers the head) and chadors (floor-length gowns). I was sure I would not be hired because I am not a Muslim. I was shown into the principal's office and interviewed by three men. I could see that the interview went well from the nodding of their heads. They thought I was qualified and liked the fact that I agreed to wear a hijab if I got the job. The following Sunday I received a call telling me that I had the job.

Several new teachers were hired that year so we were given an orientation that included the rules of the school, an introduction to Islam and assurances that we were all equal under Allah. It did not, however, take me long to realize that women were not equal to men; men made the rules. If a teacher challenged authority she was told that she could leave if she did not like it. This affected the Muslim teachers most, since they did not believe that they could be hired anywhere else. Several of the non-Muslim teachers openly challenged the wearing of the hijab. This brought the matter to the attention of the press and an open debate about religious differences, discrimination and human rights. While this was healthy in a way, its ugly side was evident when I found an anti-Christian message written in the snow that covered my car. I felt fearful, angry and powerless. I did not yet have my teaching certification and needed the job—I could not protest too loudly.

Despite other incidents, I stayed at the school for three years. I was often frustrated by the fact that I could not do what I felt was pedagogically good and morally right but in time I gained respect from the staff, the administration and the students. I learned when to be polite and deferential and when and whom I could push. These were lessons that would serve me well no matter where I taught.

Source: Adapted from Baverstock-Angelus, 1999. Reprinted with permission.

In the second case, the teacher, a young, single mother, found herself the "other" amongst her own people, in part because she tried to conform to the ways of the Cree. Betty had chosen to teach in the North as an ESL (English as a second language) teacher because she wanted to bring up her son in a quiet, unpolluted environment. Her problems were not the Cree but the other non-native teachers, who found living and working in the North very isolating.

Teaching in the Canadian North

Before I got to the North I thought that it was cold and snowy there even in the summertime. But when I got there I was amazed to find it was 27 degrees and there was lots of sand. I suddenly realized this was an ideal place to raise a child mainly because there wasn't any pollution and it was a very small community. It was like a big sandbox for him and he was in heaven.

When I first arrived in 1980, all the teachers except the kindergarten teacher were non-natives. Now most of the elementary teachers are native, though it is only recently that whites have been less in charge. I think I was prepared for the experience, not from my degree in TESL but from teaching in other countries. The other teachers were not so prepared; they prejudged the students, didn't think they were bright or talented or even capable of learning in an academic way. So it was

the teachers' biases and inexperience that made it difficult for the students. I did not get along well with the other teachers because I did not share their views. They shared their problems with each other and complained a lot about getting fresh groceries and the long waits for the cargo planes to come in.

There was another single mother who lived near me who acted as a liaison between the parents and the teachers. She understood both cultures and could translate from Cree to English and vice versa. But the other teachers refused to work with her. The animosity went both ways. When I was accepted by some of the natives, the non-natives felt I was snubbing them, so they snubbed me. It was actually a relief not to be invited to their parties, since I did not like going and no longer had to make up excuses.

I tried to incorporate Cree culture into my programs. I was the first person to put their language into the Christmas concert. I created materials that incorporated their language which helped to draw the "bush kids" back into the school after they had been out on the land hunting or fishing. I knew [that] when they came back they were in culture shock and had lost a lot of their English and fallen behind the others in school. I tried to help the other teachers understand the native way of thinking and get them to realize that their judgments came from their culture, not from the way the native people were. But they resented this.

Even though I have had difficulties in the North, it is still the place I want to go back to more than any other place. There, I feel the satisfaction and challenge as a teacher. I feel the satisfaction in making a difference in a student's life that I can't feel anywhere else.

Source: Adapted from Baverstock-Angelus, 1999. Reprinted with permission.

It is now recognized that educating a teacher is not a relatively simple and formulaic task of imparting a set of methods but rather a very complex process of developing a set of professional attitudes and a variety of strategies for coping with the many difficult encounters and situations that teachers are likely to meet in a classroom. Thus, instead of talking about teacher education or teacher training, it may be more accurate to talk about a process of *socialization* into the teaching profession.

Socialization in adulthood involves change. It involves knowing one's self. It involves confronting perhaps long-held biases and assumptions about others. For teachers, it involves a critical understanding of what is taught, why we teach what we do, how certain subjects are most effectively taught, and alternative ways of teaching. It involves making clear distinctions between classroom management considerations (discipline and order) and teaching-learning considerations. It involves being alert to the cultural as well as the political aspects of teaching. To paraphrase Bruner, what is taught, the modes of thought, and the forms of language that are promoted in schools cannot be separated from the lives and culture of the students and their teachers (1997, p. 29).

Some emphasize the idea that teacher education should focus more on the education of teachers as critical intellectuals. Giroux and McLaren (1986) in particular argue for the education of teachers as transformative intellectuals. A **transformative intellectual** is a person who exercises forms of intellectual and pedagogical practice that attempt to insert teaching and learning directly into the political sphere by arguing that schooling represents both a struggle for meaning and a struggle over power relations. We are referring to those whose intellectual practices are morally and ethically grounded in concern for the educational needs of those who have been disadvantaged and oppressed.

Giroux and McLaren state that if teachers take on the role of transformative intellectual then they will view their students as critical individuals who can question the production of knowledge as well as what knowledge is considered meaningful. Through such an approach, it is thought, students and teachers become empowered, taking the first necessary step in becoming active agents of change.

MODELS OF TEACHING

Transmission Model

Ideas about what a teacher needs to know (and, therefore, how he or she should be educated) to be able to teach effectively have undergone several revolutions, and so have views of the learner (Bruner, 1997; Hatch, 1995; Kessen, 1979). Yet, despite developments in educational psychology, which have resulted in new theories and new ways of looking at the educational process, little has changed at the level of the classroom. For example, in many parts of the world, including Canada, it used to be that teaching was seen in terms of a set of methods that could be imparted to the prospective teacher, with minor adjustments for the particular subject being taught. This **transmission model** of teacher education was premised on the assumption that learning is a fairly identifiable process, with only minor variations from one student to another, due presumably to differences either in students' intelligence or in their stage of development.

According to this model it was assumed that an entire class of twenty-five or thirty students could be taught the same material at the same pace and subsequently tested to determine how much each had learned. This view of teaching saw classrooms as uniform places where the teacher possessed the knowledge that was to be deposited into the learner. While much has changed in Western educators' thinking about teaching, classroom processes in some other parts of the world, such as Zimbabwe and Botswana, suggest that the transmission model is alive and well (Cleghorn et al., 1998; Fuller & Snyder, 1991).

Although classes have, in fact, always been diverse in terms of students' social backgrounds, temperaments, inclination to learn, family support for education, and the like, as long as they were not obviously diverse (multiracial, multicultural) then educators could behave as if the transmission model was appropriate for all learners. Once classrooms became obviously diverse, educators had to change their thinking. Unfortunately, the change was not always for the better, since the presence of "differences" sometimes provided quasi-justification for what amounted to prejudicial treatment in the classroom. Clearly such treatment did not promote learning (See Carrasco, 1981 for an example of a study on this topic).

Constructivist Model

Theoretically, we have moved far from the above view of teaching and learning to what is sometimes called the **constructivist model** or approach. According to this model, teaching is dovetailed to the cultural capital and the prior knowledge of the learners in ways that are in accord with the cultural, linguistic, and other kinds of diversity that prevail in urban centres in Canada and elsewhere. Here we use the term cultural capital in a broader than usual sense, to include the home-based ways of perceiving, thinking, speaking, believing, and behaving that all children bring to school. While the term was coined to refer to the advantage that middle-class children experience because their cultural capital corresponds to the cultural norms that dominate in the school, in a multicultural school setting with appropriately trained teachers, the cultural capital of all children should find acknowledgment.

With the civil rights movement in the United States in the 1960s, with the Quiet Revolution in Quebec (Henchey, 1987), with the vast increase in numbers of non-English- and non-French-speaking children attending schools in Canadian cities, and with an increased awareness among some educators of global issues in education, the importance of diversity and culture in the teaching-learning process came to the fore (Bruner, 1997; Grimmett, 1995; Delgado-Gaitan & Trueba, 1991).

Presently, the model of teacher education that is most prevalent in Canadian universities, for the purpose of teaching in multicultural school settings, could be characterized as **reflective practice** (Fullan & Stiegelbauer, 1991; Schön, 1983). Some term this model **social reconstructivist** (Sleeter & Grant, 1993) because it envisions a new social order that is truly equitable—one that is anti-racist (Dei, 1996), free of social class and gender bias, and preserving of ethnic diversity in and out of the classroom. Unfortunately, teacher educators and school-based personnel tend to have a limited view of what multicultural education really is, and their approach is often superficial and inadequate to effect any real change in the overall structure of society.

Ideally, the multicultural/social reconstructivist model takes into account not only a much more complex view of the learner than used to be acceptable, but a new view of the teacher. The teacher is seen as someone who has been socialized within a particular socio-cultural system, who has a multitude of taken-for-granted knowings, who is likely to be inclined to teach in the manner they themselves were taught. A great deal of what they learn about being a teacher has been absorbed throughout years as learners, observing teachers in action. There is no other profession that people observe for several hours on a nearly daily basis for twelve or more years prior to being educated to practise that profession. We believe that the importance of this extensive prior exposure to the teaching profession and to the teaching-learning process is still underestimated in its implications for teacher education.

A Constructivist-Interactionist View of Teaching

Earlier we asked if there is really a crisis in teacher education. In this section we ask if it is true, as the popular media would have it, that there is a crisis in literacy. Certainly for a society that sees close to 100 percent of its children schooled until they are 16 years of age or older, the returns on the number of years invested in their education sometimes seem to be minimal. Whatever the figures actually are (and they depend on who is counting), unacceptably large numbers of young people leave school without the skills and knowledge needed to find regular jobs. But this does not mean that the problem is one of low literacy. In fact, when we examine the statistics closely we find that children from poor, working-class and racial/ethnic minority backgrounds are overrepresented among those who struggle and sometimes fail in school (Heap, 1990). If there is a crisis, what is the nature of it? It is certainly not simply a literacy crisis.

We suggest again that there are many problems and that they are made up of many parts. Explanations offered by some educators and politically-minded school administrators tend to take the form of simplistic solutions, which find their way into the kinds of assumptions that underlie many of the remedial programs that are proposed and put in place for children at risk of school failure. The rationale for such programs is thus related to the manner in which social factors and the climate of opinion outside the classroom enter into the classroom teaching and learning process (Gumperz, 1986, p. 58).

Most remedial programs are premised upon the notion that children with difficulties in school *lack* something, both linguistically and culturally. For example, programs modeled after Headstart in the United States provide preschool training to make up for a supposed lack of verbal stimulation at home. As indicated earlier, however, there is no solid research evidence to suggest that children whose speech style deviates from the accepted (white, middle class) school standard lack the cognitive requirements for learning. What gets judged is not the child's actual ability but the manner in which that ability is displayed through interaction.

Thus, children whose language differs from the language of instruction are most often removed from the regular classroom and placed into an ESL or, as in the Province of Quebec, an FSL (French as a Second Language) classroom. When this occurs there is the likelihood that students will be exposed to language learning at the expense of learning content. These pull-out programs also tend to underestimate the learners' abilities with the result that a child is increasingly handicapped as she or he moves through the system (Flores, Cousin & Diaz, 1991).

When we analyze the above types of situations we soon come to the realization that decisions about special class placement actually have very little to do with language differences, but are rather linked more closely with established attitudes about social class, race, and ethnicity. To draw on examples from afar for a moment, the second generation children of immigrant workers in Europe are among those with the greatest problems in school, yet these children are bilingual. It is not surprising then that these are the children of people who have been systematically and officially denied access to educational and other resources in the countries they were invited to settle in as guest workers in order to provide cheap labour (Thomas, 1991). In contrast, children who are recent immigrants to North America from Asia may be far from fluent in English, yet they are "known" to do well in school (Gibson Ogbu, 1991). Thus it may be that the **social boundaries** which mark and define the differences between the dominant and minority groups in a society, through people's *perceptions* of those differences and related *expectations,* are what contribute most to success or failure in school. Stated differently, the **social meaning** attached to differences provides a definition of the situation that becomes a form of reality.

The notion of **communicative competence,** first discussed by Cazden and Hymes (1972), is important for understanding the interpretations and teacher evaluations of classroom interactions and how these affect the development of literacy and other aspects of learning. To paraphrase Gumperz (1986),

> to be effective in everyday social settings people need knowledge that goes beyond the specifics of language itself. Language usage is governed by culture, subculture and context spe-

cific norms which constrain both the choice of communicative options and the interpretation of what is said....(pp. 53–55).

Included in this process are the participants' roles, rights, and duties. In the classroom the roles of teacher and student are clearly demarcated by a power differential as well as by context-specific rules governing who can speak to whom and when. In turn, these rules find their cultural meaning and origins outside of school.

It was in this context that Susan Phillips (1972) and Jerry Lipka (1991) observed the existence of differing **participant structures** in native community classrooms in mainland United States and in Alaska, while Crago et al. (1993) have noted similar patterns in Inuit classrooms. In each case, however, all of the researchers found that when the teacher was non-native there were more student misunderstandings of what was going on and more mis-interpretations of student performance by teachers than when the teacher was native. This suggests that appropriate interpretation of the subtle cues of classroom interaction by students and by teachers depends on shared cultural understandings that go well beyond spoken language alone. Thus, teachers need to become aware of their own taken-for-granted knowledge so that this can be articulated and made explicit for children who bring different repertoires of knowledge from home to school.

In sum, if there is a crisis then it is not a crisis in teacher education and it is not a literacy crisis, per se. While change is ongoing, and it may not be clear which way to turn, it is clear that what is needed among teachers and other educators is a fuller understanding of the ways in which

> societal factors affect particular groups of children,...how and by what mechanisms they interact with schooling practices...in specific contexts to affect an individual's acquisition of reading and writing skills. That is, we must provide for the linking of explanation at the level of policy and institutional process with understanding at the more detailed level of daily educational practice (Gumperz, 1986, p. 52).

Although there have been important developments in a few scattered regions of the world and in some Canadian schools, teachers still have the same concerns: they worry about classroom management, they wonder why some children fail to learn, they are concerned with the size of their classes, and they object to out-of-class duties (Lortie, 1975). As Stigler and Stevenson (1998/99) point out, the teaching time in North American classrooms is seriously reduced by numerous interruptions and by children leaving lessons early in order to take part in extracurricular activities that are valued by school authorities as much as in-class learning. In contrast, in the Asian classrooms that these authors visited, teachers were able to complete lessons without interruption; they were observed to manage very large classes while systematically addressing a diverse range of learning needs among the students.

CURRICULUM

Curriculum refers to the courses or subjects specified by the Ministry of Education that are to be taught at each grade level as well as the amount of time to be devoted to each. In

Canada, curriculum is controlled by the provinces and territories. As a result one finds considerable variation from province to province in the extent of regulation. In some provinces, for example, the curriculum is put forth as a set of guidelines, in others there is more specificity. While the provinces generally provide lists of authorized textbooks for each subject, the decision as to which texts to use may be left up to individual school boards, schools or even teachers.

What we have just provided is a standard definition of a **formal curriculum.** Before we proceed to discuss the various debates and controversies associated with the curriculum and its implementation, it is necessary to mention what is often called the **hidden curriculum**, a term first used by Jackson (1968). The hidden curriculum refers to all those things that are taught and learned in school that are not part of the official, formal curriculum. This would include all the unwritten rules that children encounter when they first go to school. These rules have to do with such matters as order (lining up), behaviour (no running in hallways), who gets to speak when in the classroom, what constitutes fair competition, membership in an age-grade group (as contrasted to having the status of being the oldest child in the family, for example), coming and going from the classroom only at the sound of a bell, and so on. We will return to the topic of the hidden curriculum in Chapter 5 because of its role in socializing children to societal norms.

Overall, the curriculum represents a body of knowledge. If we include the curricula of programs within a university, some might think that all of the knowledge that is transmitted through educational institutions from kindergarten through university, represents the entire body of existing knowledge. This would be a mistake.

The development of school curricula in the Western world has a long history, some of it emanating from nineteenth century England, some from the United States, and some from Europe. In each case, however, most of what has been considered appropriate knowledge to be offered in schools has long ago been decided by a select group, usually composed of men who were members of an elite social class. In other words, decisions about *who* should be taught *what* have not been made by the people themselves but rather by those who believe they know what is best for teachers and students. Thus, one can see how social class and other "out-of-school" considerations enter into a discussion of curriculum. Educators, therefore, need to ask *whose* knowledge is being passed on *to whom* and *with what objectives in mind.*

It is important to realize that every curriculum represents a set of choices: some knowledge has been included, some has been left out. Some people's ideas of what is important to know have not been included. This is especially the case for visible and ethnic minorities, the disabled, and women.

Another important feature of the curricula that are found throughout the world today lies in the fact that almost everything we teach nowadays is to be found in books. Does this mean that before the printing press was invented there was no organized body of knowledge to be passed down from one generation to the next? Does this mean that in nonliterate societies there is no knowledge? The point here, again, is that *someone or a particular group has decided what knowledge is worth writing down and passing on and what knowledge is not worth passing on.* Knowledge that lends itself to *oral* transmission, the so-called *embodied* knowledge that De Castell (1990) refers to, cannot be packaged conveniently in the linear, chapter by chapter, paragraph by paragraph manner that emerged with the development of print and the widespread availability of books. This knowledge does not become part of standard curricula. What we are presented with over the years of our schooling and university education, then, is instrumental in determining how we come to view knowledge, what we consider legitimate knowledge, and what we do with it.

Curriculum Debates

It is difficult to discuss curriculum without referring directly to the role that the school plays in socialization, a topic we will expand on in Chapter 5. In this section however, we would like to draw your attention specifically to the matter of controversy over the curriculum, or curriculum debates.

In a monocultural, monolingual society, where most people share a similar ethnic or religious background, there is not likely to be much debate over the content of the curriculum. Instead, there is a wide consensus concerning what is most valued and what, therefore, should be taught in school. At most one might find disagreement about the appropriateness of religious instruction in school between those who are very religious and those who are not. But even in these circumstances, we quickly see that curriculum debates point to differences in values.

As indicated in the preceding section, the content of the curriculum is selected from a large amount of knowledge that is almost entirely written down. In Western society, although the choices have been informed by psychological and educational research that tells us what young people are capable of learning at each stage of development, curriculum remains a matter of social policy, with decisions made without either widespread consultation or agreement. That is, the decisions get made by people in positions of power, most likely people working in the Ministry of Education who have little or no background in the field of education. Therefore, what gets taught in school is political and "schools serve as arenas in which various groups will do battle for differing conceptions of what the society should value" (Apple, 1982, p. 322).

As Werner (1987) points, the curriculum debate in Canada revolves around two questions: Who should have the right to determine curriculum goals and content; and who should be involved in curriculum development, when, and how? The first question brings us back to the issue of the extent to which decision making in school governance is centralized or decentralized. That is, at what level are the goals and content decided, at the provincial level by elected officials or at the local level by teachers associations or parental interest groups? The second question raises the issue of the kind of knowledge about learning, about child development, about subject matter, and about pedagogy that is required to make informed curriculum choices.

Most of the recent debates will be familiar to the reader. Several of these are subsumed in the following questions to which there are no ready answers. We hope, however, that they will generate some lively discussions among the readers of this text, both in and out of class:

- What is the best way to teach initial reading? Phonics or whole language?
- Should literacy and numeracy (the basics) be the emphasis in the primary years?
- What kind of program will best prepare pupils for secondary schooling?
- Should religion or moral education be taught in school?
- Should art and music be included in the curriculum even when available funds are diminished?
- At what point and for what purposes should computers be introduced into the classroom?

Finally, we need to say a word about the *process of implementing a curriculum*. The first thing to remember is that a curriculum is open to interpretation. There may be a curriculum policy written down and there may be specific textbooks and other materials recommended or mandated for use, but a curriculum is implemented normally by a single teacher operating alone in a classroom with learners whose needs the teacher knows quite well. What the teacher chooses to emphasize, what she or he decides to leave out, the extent to which the teacher uses or adapts a particular text for the learners is a relatively unknown part of the curriculum equation and to that extent likely to be highly variable.

One cannot categorically say what the *learning inputs* are or what is taught on the basis of a written description of the curriculum and with the available texts and other materials at hand. One has to "look in classrooms," to borrow the title of Jackson's important book, usually over a long period of time, before one can say precisely what it is that children are taught in any particular setting, and before one can hypothesize about what might be learned.

SUMMARY/CONCLUSIONS

In this chapter, we have tried to show how discussions about the ways that teachers should be educated are closely but not perfectly related to ideas about how children should be taught. Similarly, we see that there are shifting trends in both.

Teacher education programs have moved from a direct approach model to an interactive model, and these are reflected in the two main models of teaching that we have talked about. The transmission model is characterized by whole-class, teacher-centred instruction, by a subject-oriented curriculum, and by a school day that is divided into distinct time units to correspond with the subject approach.

The constructivist model sees classrooms organized into small groups, the teaching process as student centred, the organization of time as sufficiently open to allow for a thematic approach in an otherwise integrated curriculum, and learning socially constructed through interaction.

Despite all that has been said about change in this chapter, there is a familiarity that has persisted in schools over the last fifty years or so, which still persists in classrooms throughout the world. One can walk past a tin-roofed school in rural Cameroon in West Africa and hear Shakespeare being recited, and a grade-five mathematics lesson in Zimbabwe sounds almost word for word like a grade-five mathematics lesson in a suburban Montreal school

(Cleghorn, Mtetwa, Dube & Munetsi, 1998). Children may be grouped around rectangular desks rather than seated in rows but teachers still often stand at the front of the classroom and do most of the talking (Fuller & Snyder, 1991; Prophet & Rowell, 1993).

In some classrooms, however, the power relations have shifted so that children can speak up when they do not fully understand; in others the teachers and pupils are engaged in an on-going dialogue as they try jointly to solve a problem (to construct knowledge) or devise the appropriate questions for a class research project (Stigler & Stevenson, 1997/98).

The foregoing suggests that the models of teaching which prevail today in our own schools may not really have changed much in the last generation or two. We need to ask: are young people learning more and differently in Canadian classrooms than elsewhere? Are there other effective ways of meeting diverse needs?

These are questions that require a much deeper and more critical examination than we have provided here. We hope that by the time you have finished reading this book and reflected on its contents that you will be better able to discuss these matters and to think about the direction that we might move towards.

KEY TERMS

bureaucracy	hidden curriculum	reflective practice
communicative competence	informal organization	social boundaries
constructivist model	narratives	social meaning
cultural deficits	norms	social reconstructivist
formal curriculum	open-structured schools	transformative intellectual
formal organization	participant structures	transmission model

DISCUSSION QUESTIONS

1. How would functional and conflict theorists explain the formal organization of the school? How does each perspective explain what schools teach?

2. Is there a crisis in education? If you agree that there is, what is its nature? If you disagree, can you say why?

3. List all the things that you think should be changed in (a) the ways schools are organized, (b) the ways teaching occurs. Select one or two as top priorities from each list and plan a way for the changes to take place.

RECOMMENDED READINGS/REFERENCES

Acker, S. (1988). Teachers, gender and resistance. *British Journal of Sociology of Education, 9,* 307–322.

Apple, M. (1982). *Education and power.* Boston: Routledge and Kegan Press.

Baverstock-Angelus, D. (1999). *Using teacher narratives for reflection, representation and reforms in teacher training programs.* Unpublished M.A. thesis, Concordia University, Montreal.

Blau, P., & Scott, W. R. (1962). *Formal organizations: A comparative approach.* San Fransisco: Chandler.

Bradly, J. (1994). Critical literacy, feminism, and politics of representation. In C. Lankshear, & P. Mclaren (Eds.), *Politics of liberation: Paths from Freire,* (pp.142–153). New York: Routledge.

Brock, C. (Ed.). (1996). *Global perspectives on teacher education.* Oxford studies in comparative education. Wallingford, Oxfordshire: Triangle.

Bruner, J. (1997). *The culture of education.* Massachusetts: Harvard University Press.

Carrasco, R. L. (1981). Expanded awareness of student performance: A case study in applied ethnographic monitoring in a bilingual classroom. In H.Trueba, G.P. Guthrie, & K. H-P. Au (Eds.), *Culture and the bilingual classroom* (pp. 153–177). Rowley: Newbury House Publishers.

Cazden, C., & Hymes, D. (Eds.). (1972). *Functions of language in the classroom.* New York: Teachers College Press.

Cleghorn, A., & Genesee, F. (1984). Languages in contact: An ethnographic study of interaction in an immersion school. *TESOL Quarterly, 18* (4), 595–625.

Cleghorn, A., Mtetwa, D., Dube, R. & Munetsi, C. (1998). Classroom language use in multilingual settings: Mathematics lessons from Quebec and Zimbabwe. *International Journal of Qualitative Studies in Education, 11* (3), 463–477.

Corwin, R. G. (1965). *A sociology of education.* New York: Appleton-Century Crofts.

Crago, M., Annahatak, B., & Ningiuruvik, L. (1993). Changing patterns of language socialization in Inuit homes. *Anthropology and Education Quarterly, 24*(3), 205–223.

Culley, M. & Portuges, C. (1985). *Gendered Subjects: The dynamics of feminist teaching.* Boston: Routledge & Keegan Paul.

De Castell, S. (1990). Defining significant knowledge: Some limits to literacy. In S. P. Norris, & L. M. Phillips (Eds.). *Foundations of literacy policy in Canada* (pp.23–36). Calgary: Detselig.

Dei, G. (1996). Black/African-Canadian student's perspectives on school racism. In M. I. Alladin (Ed.), *Racism in Canadian schools* (pp.42–57). Toronto: Harcourt Brace.

Delgado-Gaitan, C., & Trueba, H. (1991). *Crossing cultural borders: Education for immigrant families in America.* New York: Falmer Press.

Dickinson, G. (1987). The legal dimensions of teachers' duties and authority. In R. Ghosh, & D. Ray (Eds.), *Social change and education in Canada* (pp. 210–230). Toronto: Harcourt Brace Jovanovish,

Flores, B., Cousin, P., & Dias, E. (1991). Transforming deficit myths about learning language and culture. *Language Arts, 68,* 369–379.

Fullan, M., & Stiegelbauer, S. (1991). *The new meaning of educational change.* Toronto:OISE Press.

Fuller, B., & Snyder, C. W. (1991). Vocal teachers, silent pupils: Life in Botswana classrooms. *Comparative education review, 35* (2), 274–294.

Ghosh, R., & Ray, D. (Eds.) (1987). *Social change and education in Canada.* (1st ed.). Toronto: Harcourt Brace Jovanovish.

Ghosh, R., & Ray, D. (Eds.). (1995). *Social change and education in Canada.* (3rd ed.). Toronto: Harcourt Brace.

Gibson, M. A., & Ogbu, J. U. (Eds.), (1991). *Minority Status and Schooling.* New York: Garland Publishing.

Giroux, H., & McLaren, P. (1989). *Critical pedagogy, the state and cultural struggle.* Albany: State University of New York Press.

Goodlad, J. (1990). *Teachers for our nation's schools.* San Fransisco: Jossey-Bass.

Grimmett, P. P., & Wideen, M. (Eds.). (1995). *Changing times in teacher education.* London: Falmer Press.

Greenberger, E., & Sorensen, A. (1970). Interpersonal choices among a junior high school faculty. *Sociology of education, 44,* 198–216.

Grimmett, P. P., & Wideen, M.(Eds.). (1995). *Changing times in teacher education.* London: Falmer Press.

Gumperz, J. J. (1986). Interactional sociolinguistics in the study of schooling. In J. Cook-Gumperz (Ed.), *The social construction of literacy* (pp. 45–68). Cambridge: Cambridge University Press.

Hatch, A. (Ed.). (1995). *Qualitative research in early childhood settings.* Connecticut: Praeger.

Heap, J. L. (1990). Effective functioning in daily life: A critique of concepts and surveys of functional literacy. In S. P .Norris,. & L. M. Phillips, (Eds.), *Foundations of literacy policy in Canada* (pp. 37–52). Calgary: Detselig.

Henchey N. (1987). The ew technology and the transformation of learning. In R. Ghosh ,& D. Ray.(Eds.), *Social change and education in Canada* (pp. 42–56.). Toronto: Harcourt Brace,

Holmes Group (1986). *Tomorrow's teachers.* East Lansing: Holmes Group.

Jackson, P. (1968). *Life in classrooms.* New York: Holt, Rinehart & Winston.

Kessen, W. (1979). The American child and other cultural inventions. *American Psychologist, 34,* 815–820.

Laird, S. (1988). Reforming 'women's true profession': A case for 'feminist pedagogy' in teacher education? *Harvard Educational Review, 58* (4), 449–463.

Levin, B., & Young, J. (1994). *Understanding Canadian schools: An introduction to educational administration.* Toronto: Harcourt Brace.

Lipka, J. (1991). Toward a culturally based pedagogy: A case study of one Yup'ik eskimo teacher. *Anthropology and Education Quarterly, 22,* 203–223.

Lortie, D. (1975). *Schoolteacher.* Chicago: University of Chicago Press.

Martin, J. R. (1985). *Reclaiming a conversation: The ideal of the educated woman.* New Haven: Yale University Press.

Martin, W. B. W. (1975). The negotiated order of teachers in team teaching situations. *Sociology of Education, 48,* 202–222.

Martin, W. B. W. (1976). *The negotiated order of the school.* Toronto: MacMillan.

Martin, W. B. W. & Macdonell, A. (1978). *Canadian Education.* Toronto: Prentice Hall.

Norris, S., & Phillips, L. (1990). *Foundations of literacy policy in Canada.* Calgary: Detselig.

Phillips, S. U. (1972). Participant structures and communicative competence: Warm springs children in community and classroom. In C. Cazden, V. John, & D. Hymes (Eds.), *Functions of language in the classroom (*pp. 370–394).New York: Teachers College Press,.

Prophet, R. B., & Rowell, P. M .(1993). Coping and control: Science teaching strategies in Botswana. *International Journal of Qualitative Studies in Education, 6* (3), 197–209.

Rich, A. (1985). Taking women students seriously. In M. Culley, & C. Portuges (Eds.), *Gendered subjects: The dynamics of feminist teaching.{Q: page numbers?}* Boston: Routledge and Kegan Paul.

Schön, D. (1983). *The reflective practitioner.* London: Temple Smith.

Shrewsbury, C. M. (1987). What is feminist pedagogy? *Women's Studies Quarterly, 15*, (Nos. 3–4).pp. 6–14.

Sleeter, C. E., & Grant, C. A. (1993). *Making choices for multicultural education.* Toronto: Maxwell Macmillan Canada.

Spencer, M. (1979). *The foundations of modern sociology.*(2nd ed.) Englewood Cliffs, N.J.: Prentice Hall

Stigler, J. W., & Stevenson, H. W. (1998/99). How Asian teachers polish each lesson to perfection. In E.J. Nunn, & C. J. Boyatzis. *Child growth and development* (pp. 90–101). Guilford, Connecticut: McGraw-Hill.

Tabulawa, R. (1998). Teachers' perspectives on classroom practice in Botswana: Implications for pedagogical change. *International Journal of Qualitative Studies in Education 11* (2), 249–268.

Thomas, R. M. (Ed.). (1990). International comparative education: *Practices, issues and prospects.* New York: Pergamon.

Trueba, H., Guthrie, G. P., & Au Hu-Pei, K. (1981). *Culture and the bilingual classroom.* Rowley: Newbury House Publishers.

Tulasiewicz, W. (1996). Is there a crisis in teacher education?. In C. Brock, (Ed.) *Global perspectives on teacher education* (pp. 19–34). Oxford studies in comparative education. Wallingford, Oxfordshire: Triangle.

Weber, S., & Mitchell, C. (1995). *That's funny, you don't look like a teacher!: interrogating images and identity in popular cultures.* Washington, D. C.: Falmer Press

Werner, W. (1987). Curriculum and socialization. In R. Ghosh, & D. Ray (Eds.), *Social change and education in Canada* (pp. 91-101). Toronto: Harcourt Brace Jovanovich.

Werner, W. (1995). Persistent curriculum issues. In R. Ghosh, & D. Ray Eds.), *Social change and education in Canada.* (3rd ed.) (pp. 126–136).Toronto: Harcourt Brace.

CRITICAL PERSPECTIVES ON THE POLITICS OF TEACHING AND PEDAGOGY

Chapter **4**

Chapter Objectives

The purpose of this chapter is to clarify the distinction between teaching and pedagogy. To do so we build on the theories presented in Chapter 2, providing a detailed account of critical pedagogy and feminist pedagogy. We show that both pedagogies were generated from the work of Paulo Freire. A study that illustrates the implementation of critical pedagogy into classroom practice is then presented; this stands as an example of what is possible when educators fully understand the political nature of the schooling process. This is followed by a discussion of feminist pedagogy and how it attempts to go further than critical pedagogy to work towards changing class, race, and gender inequities.

THE POLITICS OF TEACHING

Teachers bring to the schooling situation a great deal of both commonsense and taken-for-granted knowledge. This knowledge has been acquired not only during their formal teacher education but also during their own socialization within the same sociocultural system in which they later on teach. For example, the idea that schools, organized in traditional, familiar ways are appropriate places for students to learn, generally goes unquestioned. Similarly, we all have been influenced by the belief that we live in a meritocracy, where individual effort and ability lead to higher educational achievement. These beliefs are bound up with what we have earlier referred to as society's dominant ideology.

Ideology is commonly taken to mean a set of beliefs and values held by a group (or a society), usually based on an interpretation of the past with prescriptions of policy for the future. For Marx, ideology refers to a belief system that legitimates the dominant group. He maintains that this system is generated and controlled by the owners of material production. In other words, the economic dominance of the ruling class controls the world of ideas as well. Marx's conceptualization is of value because it grounds ideology in material experience and observable human behaviour, but it becomes problematic insofar as it implies that societal ideas and beliefs are deliberately manipulated in a calculated way so as to indoctrinate the subordinate class. According to Marx ideology serves the powerful group by presenting the powerless or subordinate groups with a definition of reality that is false; as this definition becomes part of the shared belief system it provides order to the surrounding world.

Weber (1947) broadens Marx's notion of ideology to include how ideology and control are more powerful and effective when they are cloaked in beliefs that make it appear legitimate through the educational system. For Weber, one of the major roles of an education system is to disseminate the dominant ideology through the populace.

Later development of these ideas came from Gramsci's concept of hegemony, which shows how ideology originates and operates in a subtle fashion as a kind of preponderance of influence. The hegemonic aspect of ideology arises from its ability to build social consensus by appealing to a selective interpretation of the past and people's commonsense assumptions about the world. For instance, the genesis of the myth of the "American dream" stems from the success stories of a minority of new Americans, with the Puritan ethos of hard work serving as an explanation for their success. After industrialization and the advent of institutionalized education for all in the nineteenth century, this ideology was translated into educational values. The reward for hard work in school was translated into the achievement of a higher social status. Individual success stories, however, such as that of Henry Ford in the U.S. and Samuel Bronfman in Canada, can be cited as evidence of the fact that the accumulation of fortune was not necessarily linked to educational credentials.

Ideology is a dynamic rather than a static mechanism; it is a living belief that is bound up with and brought to life in the consciousness of the student, shaping his or her perception of self and society in many significant ways. From within the institution of the school, the dominant ideology affects and develops the consciousness of the student, shaping his or her perception of self and society in many significant ways. Education is not merely a distant mechanism for sorting and selecting individuals for the work world; the institution operates as such because people have come to believe that this is part of the school's task. That is, education aids in the reproduction of this ideology; schools reproduce social and economic inequality by perpetuating patterns of success and failure, which, as already stated, go unquestioned since they are considered "normal." The primary institution for controlling ideology is the school. This is what is meant by the politics of teaching and education.

When institutionalized ways of doing things become part of the intrapsychic make-up of the individual, the system supports the dominant group. The primary institution where these mechanisms of control are played out, passed on, and perpetuated, then, is the school.

TEACHING AND PEDAGOGY

In this section we further examine how the politics of education finds its way into pedagogical practice. As Roger Simon (1987) notes, **pedagogy** refers to the production of knowledge, identities, and values; it must, therefore, be distinguished from teaching.

> Pedagogy [refers] to the integration in practice of particular curriculum content and design, classroom strategies and techniques, and evaluation, purpose and method. All of these aspects organize a view of how a teacher's work within an institutional context specifies a particular version of what knowledge is most worth, what it means to know something, and how we might construct representations of ourselves, others, and our physical and social environment...(p.370)

The shift away from teaching, the transmission of knowledge, to pedagogy, the production of knowledge, has led researchers to look on pedagogy as a form of cultural politics. By cultural politics we mean that those in positions of power determine such matters as curriculum. That is, those in power determine what others ought to and, perhaps, may learn. If, for example, those who make the decisions consider computers to be more important than, say, art or music, then computers will win out. Simon further states,

> In other words, talk about pedagogy is simultaneously talk about the details of what students and others might do together and the cultural politics such practices support. In this perspective, we cannot talk about teaching practices without talking about politics. (p.370).

Simon (1987) and Giroux (1989), drawing on Freire's work, use a critical perspective to view culture not only as a way of life but as a form of production that involves relations of power and legitimization of certain meanings and experience.

Paulo Freire: Liberation through Education

Freire's primary concern was with social transformation and with developing an emanicpatory or liberatory education. He explains how this process can occur by focusing on educational practices, the empowerment of teachers, teachers as agents of empowering students, and social class empowerment. Much of his work has been regarded as highly political and has become the foundation for the development of a new more liberating pedagogy.

Since both the critical and feminist pedagogists were greatly influenced by Paulo Freire, it is useful to discuss his views in some detail. First, however, it is important to note that Freire's philosophy reflects the societal conditions in Brazil, the country that he came from and was most familiar with. That is, his experience was first with an impoverished society, where there was a huge gap between a small, wealthy, and educated elite and a large, extremely poor, and uneducated peasant class. Nevertheless, Freire speaks to and is heard by all who have experienced oppression, as well as by those who are concerned with increasing equality.

Freire (1968) aimed to develop a **theory of liberation** that could provide a basis for educational theory and practice. For him, it is not only people who are processed in schools but also knowledge that is selected, organized, and then processed, too. Freire believes that individuals have the power to come to an understanding of their own situation in the world. He refers to this as critical consciousness. It is important to note that Freire believes that both teachers and students are agents engaged in constructing and reconstructing meaning. That is, they are agents who could transform educational practice.

Freire's theory of liberation attempted to provide a basis for educational theory and practice in the radical sense, by focusing on social change and fracturing the status quo, and to bridge these dichotomous strands of pedagogy. Thus researchers must ask questions about the selection and organization of knowledge. They must treat knowledge, or what counts as knowledge, as socially constructed. That is, researchers need to explore how and why certain dominant categories of knowledge persist, how they link with certain interests and occupational groups, and understand the influence of the elite's traditions. Freire asks if educators cannot change the criteria of high-class knowledge so that it is concrete rather than abstract, oral rather than literate, communal rather than individual. That is, Freire is seeking ways to make the accepted (upper-class) knowledge accessible to the peasant and working classes.

Freire views education as a radical project for economic, political, and cultural change in which power relations are transformed. Pedagogy (classroom management, teaching style, classroom activities, evaluation) is the means or process by which curriculum (subject content, knowledge) is communicated. All pedagogy, therefore, is essentially political.

Culture and Schooling

In this section, we look at Freire's view of culture and schooling and link it to his theory for achieving social change via education. Freire sees the function of culture as more than passing on a heritage: Its function is political. The dominant culture functions to legitimize existing modes of social relations and production. It also functions to provide the motivational structures that link individual needs with social needs. Furthermore, culture provides a society with the symbolic language for interpreting the boundaries of individual and social existence.

Freire is concerned not only with making knowledge accessible to the poor and other oppressed people, but he also wants to transform pedagogy so that the views of the elite change as well. He thus diverges from the standard, deterministic view of pedagogy to suggest that new understandings can be constructed by the higher classes even though their perceptions of social reality may differ from those who are oppressed. That is, Freire does not see schools in purely mechanistic terms. Schools do not simply process students for the realms of leisure and work.

Freire places ideology within the sphere of individual consciousness. Ideology shapes people's perceptions of reality, which are defined by the dominant classes who control educational access, processes, and content. But there is passivity among the oppressed. Pedagogical practices are thus saturated with mechanisms to maintain the position of the elite with the result that those who do not have control are robbed of the possibility of developing a critical consciousness. That is, what teaching and knowledge they do receive ensures that they remain passive. This Freire refers to as the **culture of silence.**

By suggesting that ideology is part of consciousness, Freire views it as a contradictory force because consciousness is composed not only of the dominant ideology but also of critical, good sense. In this way, consciousness is characterized by a constant struggle between people's capacity to think critically and the power of hegemonic ideology. This struggle within our consciousness is revealed through **dialogue**. The purpose of dialogue is not only to validate the voices and subjective experiences of the oppressed but also to expose both the subjective and the objective nature of ideology, that is, the beliefs and practices that influence our thoughts and action. By critiquing our thoughts through dialogue, we begin to carve out a path towards becoming critically conscious actors engaged in the construction of a more humane world.

The kind of dialogue that Freire had in mind relates to the concrete situations and lived experiences that inform daily our lives. This kind of dialogue leads to the recognition of one's own cultural capital and how it can be used to reclaim one's own identity. This pedagogy does not teach reading and writing passively. It is a pedagogy that questions. The content of instruction must, then, be rooted in the cultural capital of learners and made problematic through critical dialogue.

Briefly then, students have to learn how culture functions in the interest of the dominant classes. They must examine the form and content of the approved texts to reveal the ideologies, images, and ideas they present. The words, setting, and images contained in school materials have to be examined, their political implications and social consequences noted. Through such analysis, students come to see that they can engage in social and political reconstruction. That is, a means for promoting critical comprehension of contradictory cultural meanings and practices is developed.

Concept of Dialogue

The dialogue form of pedagogy presupposes that the student and teacher are equals; both are subjects in a world characterized by ideological and structural forces that shape and influence thought and action. In order for dialogue to be successful in recovering, validating, and critiquing the experiences of students, then, teachers must not impose knowledge on students as in the traditional manner of "banking" education. Banking education occurs when teachers consider students to be empty receptacles, which they are to fill with knowledge. When teachers approach education this way, students then memorize this knowledge, yet rarely question or analyze it to reveal its underlying interests.

Pedagogy that takes a dialogical form seeks not only to question the knowledge that students learn in school, but also to validate the knowledge that students already possess, that which they gain from experiencing life as a particular individual, in a particular historical and social circumstance. Stated another way, individuals are not merely passive receptors of knowledge and ideology. Rather, they are always mediating these by commonsense and their own identities, which are shaped by their class, race, ethnicity, and gender. The exploration of the subjective experiences, thus, also reveals the choices and the actions that individuals make to counter or resist the forces that seek to shape and limit them.

Perception of Knowledge

For Freire, liberation means being able to construct your own meanings, frame of reference, and self-determining powers through an ability to understand reality. Knowledge is not neutral: It is generated from human activity situated in norms and interests. The act of knowing is more than a technical issue—it is a political issue. Under the guise of objectivity, knowledge has been used to legitimate belief and value systems. "Objective" knowledge mystifies and turns people into spectators by removing underlying norms, values, and interests from public debate.

Not only do we need to demystify knowledge, but we must also question the processes used to constitute and legitimate knowledge and experience. How can this be accomplished? We must transcend the realms of intellectual habit and commonsense. Radical educators must learn to highlight and make problematic the knowledge they present to their students, and to question meaning and the nature of knowledge itself. For instance, they should be asking, Whose reality is being legitimated by this knowledge? Whose interest does this knowledge represent? Why is it being taught this way? Does this knowledge have meaning for the learner? Is this knowledge part of the learners' cultural capital? Knowledge, then, must become the mediator of communications and dialogue.

Conscientization/Critical Consciousness

Conscientization is the term used by Friere to refer to an awakening process. The path towards critical consciousness or conscientization involves a reinterpretation of what is considered to constitute knowledge. It indicates that individuals exist not only *in* the world but also *with* the world. We cannot separate ourselves from our own personal world, nor can we separate ourselves from the structural and ideological barriers of the external world.

This dialectical view provides a basis by which individuals cannot only become conscious but, most importantly, critically conscious and, ultimately, act to create a more humane world. The difference between the two sides of consciousness lies in the ability to decipher how societal forces, both ideological and structural, enable and limit individuals. An inability to analyze these forces and link them to dominating interests means that an individual has not developed a critical consciousness but is still at the stage of what Freire refers to as "native consciousness" (1985). At this stage, the individual is considered a determined being because although she or he possesses a consciousness it is not his or her own but that of his or her oppressor.

As part of the subject-object dialectic, knowledge is crucial to the liberation of oppressed individuals; they will come to know that it is a social construction and that they can participate in its construction. In the classroom, critical consciousness involves not only the validation of the knowledge-based experiences that individuals bring to school with them but also a simultaneous critique of school knowledge. A critique of school knowledge demystifies the supposed objectivity of knowledge and its links to the interests of dominant groups.

An understanding that knowledge is socially constructed and never complete forms part of the process of empowerment of disenfranchised individuals. In other words, knowledge gives people power. When students' subjective experiences are acknowledged and incorporated through dialogue into the learning process, students gain voice.

Schools as Centres of Liberating Praxis

According to Freire, schools are centres of **praxis** (reflection and action) where social change can occur. It is in schools where a multiplicity of personal, subjective experiences come together under conditions of supposed equality. Yet, education rarely entails questioning the knowledge that it teaches for its own underlying interests, nor validates the knowledge that students bring into the classroom. In this way, education maintains the status quo and is seen as a profoundly political process.

Inherent in any educational design are value assumptions about the nature of humankind and specific forms of knowledge. These notions, validating certain subjective understandings of experience while devaluing others, are passed down through pedagogy and reinforced in the minds of students.

Defined by its ideologies and practices, the politics of education can be as liberating as it is constraining. Schooling practices that shape the individual and collective consciousness of students can be questioned. Issues of power relations between individuals and society can be addressed. School knowledge can be critiqued. The student's perception of her or his oppression can be validated. Briefly, the power of hegemonic ideology can be overcome in schools. Schools can be centres for change because it is here that the individual can begin to learn that she or he can participate in the organization of his or her society.

Critiques of Freire

One criticism of Freire's work is that it is situation specific. That is, Freire's pedagogy is thought to be aimed too much at the liberation of oppressed populations in underdeveloped nations. It is true that oppression of the kind existing in underdeveloped nations may not be as prevalent in the developed nations. This criticism, however, does not dismiss the fact that the more developed countries are also characterized by domination and oppression, albeit of a more subtle variety. Thus, Freire's pedagogy cannot be imposed in a grid-like way but must be altered to take into consideration the varying forms of oppression and domination in our unique historical and social context.

Another critique centres on the idea that domination is legitimized through the dominant ideology, which permeates all levels of society. There are different forms of legitimization. We must clarify how the legitimization of domination has been applied in schools so as to obscure political interests. For example, science and technology are used to conceal class-specific interests and values (Aikenhead, 1990). Freire does not account for this. His notion of ideology must be developed to address the legitimization and socialization process in schools in modern industrialized countries.

In clarifying Freire's concept of ideology we must also go beyond the material and psychological forces that sustain ideologies to include the historical forms of political and social life that produce them. That is, the social composition of the political forces at work in these dominated societies must be identified. We have to account for the organizational and mobilization capacities of the social groups involved before Freire's vision of social transformation can be considered as viable.

Another concept which needs to be further developed is dialogical communication. We must ask if we can clarify the intended and unintended consequences of the hidden curriculum through dialogical communication. Freire assumes that in battling oppression the oppressed will move towards humanization. The oppressed, however, can become the oppressor once their oppressive conditions have been overcome. Freire's response to this criticism has been that individuals must engage in self-critique and question their assumptions and practices in order to understand how their actions can also become oppressive.

Finally, Freire appears to create an illusion of equality amongst the oppressed, in terms of their experiences as well as their conception of a more humane society. The oppressed cannot be considered a homogeneous group, even if they are all experiencing one common form of oppression. Individuals who are oppressed may experience within-group forms of oppression, which will alter their vision of how a more humane society ought to be organized.

Despite these critiques, Freire's pedagogy cannot and has not been dismissed. In the following sections we examine the work of a number of critical and feminist pedagogists who were influenced by Freire.

CRITICAL PEDAGOGY

Critical pedagogy is fundamentally concerned with understanding the relationship between power and knowledge. Knowledge is socially constructed and deeply rooted in power relations. Critical pedagogy asks how and why knowledge gets constructed the way it does and how and why some constructions of reality are legitimated by the dominant culture, while others are not. It asks, then, what are the social functions of knowledge (McLaren, 1998).

The dominant culture is able to exercise control through the process of hegemony, in which the powerful gain the compliance of the oppressed in perpetuating their own oppression. Hegemony is supported by ideology, whether that be the ideology of communism, socialism, or capitalism, and permeates all of social life. We use ideology to "make sense" of our world. When ideology is queried we come to understand which concepts, values, and meanings obscure, or, alternatively, clarify our understanding of our place within the world.

Resistance

The work of Giroux (1983; 1989; 1996), Weiler (1988; 1991) and Willis (1977) on resistance among youth subcultures illustrates the practical applications of critical pedagogy in educational practice. Youth subcultures infiltrate schools, creating profound effects on student motivation, classroom management, academic standards, school discipline, and safety. That is, they constitute a problem requiring a more concerted response than simple disciplinary measures. The challenge is to find ways to harness the resistance of these groups so that they remain within the system and become more willing participants in it. This is thought to be possible if they share in the power relations and if their experience is given voice. That is, if they are permitted to contribute to the meaning of the knowledge that they themselves construct. By understanding the reason for their emergence, the structure and the purpose of these subcultures, educators may be able to embrace these youths as allies in the learning process.

One particular explanation for the emergence of youth subcultures has to do with the notion of resistance. **Resistance** is defined as any behaviour, passive or active, that goes beyond simply opposing one or many elements of the dominant group. To evaluate the degree of resistance, both the quality as well as the consequences of the resistant behaviour must be taken into account (Giroux, 1983). Youth subcultures frequently offer the adolescent the opportunity for resistance against the prevailing power structure, which in schools is clearly demarcated between teachers and administrators, who are in positions of power and control, and students, who form a subordinate group with little actual say in what happens to them for several hours each day. As Weiler (1988) points out, the ideology that supports the system of control over the subordinate group is a system of values, morals, and beliefs, or a structure of thought and consciousness that frames the individual's perception and experience of the world. Giroux's (1983) analysis of resistance includes the individual's needs, history, and subjectivity as well as the individual's ability to act, struggle, and critique on a personal and political level both self and society. He notes that an opportunity to resist may lead certain youths to a new consciousness and recognition regarding their place in the social structure. It is this behaviour, which opposes the status quo, out of reach of those formerly in control, that is deemed to be a problem. Individual members within a resisting youth subculture understand that they are not passive recipients of domination, but, rather, active agents engaged in negotiation, mediation, and alteration of personal and collective meanings, capable of transforming their environments (Giroux, 1983). Resistance cannot be just the rejection of a dominant value, neither can it be an acceptance of submission or a partial uncovering of the dominance. Resistance must lead to a change in the hegemonic ideology. Such change may only come with a fully developed critical consciousness, a result of praxis (reflection and action) (Freire, 1968), which involves not only the youth but the teachers and the other adults in their lives. Freire's praxis involves the power of the individual to act as an agent of change to create and recreate meaning.

Praxis allows the individual to understand the limitations of the environment and uncover the means to resist these very limitations. The reflective period leads to some form of action with an intent to transform and change the environment. By "naming, reading and knowing reality"(Weiler, 1988, p. 18), the individual challenges the received vision of reality and appropriates a personal vision. Such a critique of hegemonic ideologies via reflection-action-reflection can lead to social transformation.

By questioning situations, traditions, history, and their own life world (intellectual, emotional, and physical space), students can be taught to think critically and move towards liberation. This type of teaching, known as critical pedagogy, succeeds best when the multiple subjectivities of both teacher and student are included in the classroom and when the students themselves present the conflicts and issues that are discussed and explored. The development of a critical consciousness occurs in three stages: intransitive thought (fatalistic); semitransitive (some hope for change); and critical transitivity, or praxis (dynamic relationship between thought and action). This approach is particularly effective when used by teachers working with resistant youths who feel disempowered. We would suggest, however, that it not be viewed simply as a remedial strategy, but that it belongs in all classrooms; if used more often, it might go a long way towards preventing resistant youth subcultures from forming.

Paul Willis' 1977 study *Learning to Labour,* carried out in England, is one of the most influential on the topic of resistance. The study showed how class culture is reproduced and how working-class boys resisted the dominant ideology and power that were imposed on them. These working-class boys, or "lads," as they were referred to by Willis, rejected the ideology of the school, that is, the class-tainted values and the knowledge embedded in the curriculum, which was offered without mediation in respect to the cultural capital that working-class children bring to school. From the boys' perspective, the school rejected their working-class culture, the characteristics of which they chose to emphasize as a strategy of resistance. They rejected and actively resisted the values and knowledge of the school, which they viewed as imposed on them. Indeed, they saw manual work as productive, and mental work as destructive to maintaining their working-class culture. However, their resistance to schooling and their emphasis on their own class culture did not lead them out of their genuinely oppressive conditions. Rather, the social boundary between their position and the position of those in control was solidified. Thus, in a way, their resistance was an indication of their complicity in remaining where they were. The following case study illustrates the practical application of critical pedagogy in a school where youths have resisted the norms and values of traditional schools.

The Alternate School

The Alternate School is an alternative secondary school aimed at helping at-risk and troubled students in a small setting of 65–75 students. The school is for students who have dropped out of regular school, or are deemed to be dysfunctional or delinquent. These students have experienced social and personal difficulties that have interfered with their academic success (i.e., conduct disorders such as temper control and impulsiveness; sexual crises, such as rape, incest, abuse,and teen pregnancy; substance abuse, such as alcohol, food, and drug abuse; and delinquencies, such as prostitution, gang membership, living on the street, armed robbery, assault, and drug trafficking). The students at The Alternate School are considered troubled adolescents and categorized into various levels of delinquency, which is considered a normal, natural entry requirement of the school. These are youths who have resisted the traditional educational system and are in search of an alternative route.

By existing within the traditional education system of Quebec, but practising outside this system, The Alternate School is transformed from an authoritarian, anti-intellectual, passive, teacher-talk model of education to the one proposed by Freire, as described by McLaren and Leonard (1993). This model is democratic, intellectually challenging, student active, and emancipatory. According to the tenets of critical pedagogy, the philosophy of The Alternate School is founded on mutual respect and equality. These are not simply empty words; they are put into action daily. The traditional approach, where the teacher is the authority, always right, and has certain inalienable rights, does not exist at The Alternate School. From cleaning toilets together to discussing courses of discipline, from structuring examinations to designing curriculum, teachers and students perform the same tasks as a team. Staff and classroom decisions are made after extensive dialogue takes place and a consensus is achieved. This democratic atmosphere encourages these students to see themselves as active agents of change

(Giroux, 1983). Through the process of dialogue and consensus, students are encouraged to question the rules, contest the decisions, and redefine their situations. That is, their voices are heard.

When students enter The Alternate School, they have already experienced and resisted certain limitations within their environment. They have understood that simple oppositional behaviours (i.e., skipping classes, verbally assaulting teachers, and avoiding homework) do not change situations; they realize that, if anything, this behaviour worsens their situation. Students who demonstrate oppositional behaviour in regular schools contradict the everyday social order of the school for a limited period of time, but, eventually, most of them fade back into the mainstream.

Through their problems, students who resist the traditional education system find solutions that require action. Their resistant behaviour offers them a sense of freedom from the dominance of a system that they feel does not work for them. After a period of reflection, when they may view their situation as problematic because it is affecting their lives, the students move toward action, either by withdrawing from the system, by existing independently in the system, or by counterresisting.

The first action officially required of the students is to make the initial contact with The Alternate School. Students must refer themselves to the school by making a telephone call to establish an interview time. This first step is critical, for it indicates that they are attempting to take charge of their situation and make changes. It shows that they have left behind the fatalistic and hopeless voice of intransitive thinking and have moved into a stage of semitransitive thought, as outlined in Giroux's (1983) description of critical consciousness. It is this stage that is the key to success in the students' experience at the school. At this point in the students' lives, the particular issues related to mainstream schooling have become problematic. Through the process of questioning and evaluating, the students reach the conclusion that change must occur. They redefine their situations and see the possibilities for a new reality. The phone call is the first step for change.

As much as schools make youths feel powerless and submissive, this phone call has the opposite effect. It signals to youths that the everyday social order can change. Following the first or second interview, students spend a trial period in the school so that they may determine if the school is appropriate for them. This second phase in the entry procedure places the power for change, once again, in the students' hands. After this trial period, students have the choice to leave the school and seek out something elsewhere that benefits them. For those students who choose to stay, the third phase is a probationary period, a period of time when students participate fully in classes and school life. Students who choose to remain at the school are those who have already experienced a discrepancy between "what is and what is supposed to be." A desire to change self and system is the motivation common amongst these students. This common perspective instantly unites many students into the role of human agents of change, capable of transforming their environments. Students spend much of their one-year stay at the school in one of two stages: semitransitive thought, whereby they demonstrate some hope for change, or critical transitive thought, whereby they demonstrate a strong, positive dynamic between thought and action.

These patterns of thought and action are resistant behaviours because they empower students to understand their place in the hierarchy and to transform the existing social structure. For instance, Mary, a 14-year-old female who left an abusive relationship with her 26-year-old boyfriend, volunteers at a battered woman's shelter to gain back her control and fight against the system. Liz, an 18-year-old female fighting anorexia nervosa, runs seminars in elementary classrooms about the ravaging effects of the disease. Tim, a 19-year-old male, actively speaks out against sexual abuse when he recounts the effects of a male rape he experienced at the age of 14. Adam, a 17-year-old male, resists the wave of family violence he experienced and donates his time and photographic talent to an urban organization that works to combat youth street violence. All these examples show how students who understand the source of their struggle can see active solutions within their problems and extract meaning from their environments.

Critical Consciousness

The students at The Alternate School share certain values. Because the mode of instruction at the school is cooperative and interactive, students immediately begin to talk about their ideas, thoughts, and feelings with their peers and teachers. Because an atmosphere of democracy and equality prevails, students are free to express their opinions. They are challenged to step forward and take responsibility for themselves, for the group, and for the social conditions at the school. Social problems, such as homelessness, the abuse of women, and the use of weapons, become the focus of class discussions in which the students initiate projects that address these problems on both a personal and a social level. Projects such as serving meals to the homeless, volunteering time at a women's shelter, and participating in the annual Amnesty Weapons Day help students to assert their leadership skills, activate their compassion (often dormant in troubled adolescents), and distance themselves from their personal crises. Furthermore, when these students are enmeshed in the neighbourhood and bonded to the community, their delinquent acts are reduced; it is difficult for them to perform destructive acts on individuals who are known to them, who are not faceless individuals.

As the first step in helping students to develop their thinking processes, teachers are asked to "suspend personal belief biases" (Bibby & Posterski, 1992, p. 16). To understand the student perspective, teachers must first examine their own biases. Teachers at The Alternate School are reminded that, when working with negative youth subcultures, the starting point of learning, discussion, and change may be more important than

where the process ends. Activities must originate from the students themselves, who are taught to think about, discuss, and tackle issues using a six-step process that is presented in question format.

1. What is the actual content of the issue?
2. Who is presenting the issue, and how does this impact on the truth of the issue?
3. How do I know what I know?
4. How is this issue like something else/unlike something else I know?
5. To whom would this issue be relevant and why?
6. Why bother looking at the issue in the first place?

Using this approach, students are asked to look past the superficial. They are asked to analyze the deeper meaning of the social issue, understand its context, determine its relevancy, and articulate a response in their own voice. Students are taught to understand their actions and to link these to the actions of others. They see that their choices are directly tied to the limitations of others. For example, Black students were recently discussing the problems that they face when entering local stores. They expressed anger at immediately being scrutinized by store owners. Linking this experience to the study of the historical oppression of Black Americans and the civil rights struggles of the 1960s, students were shocked to see that, in their view, very little had changed since then. They understood the effects that affirmative action and gaining the right to vote had, but saw that difficulties still exist on both a personal and a societal level.

Generative Themes

Critical pedagogy requires that students assert themselves, see the inequalities of the social order, tackle the injustices of domination, and uncover the politics of education. Freire (1968) suggests that it is the duty and moral obligation of teachers to become problem posers and present thought-provoking subjects based on social issues relevant to student life. Teachers, by using student vocabulary, lead the students to reflect on social issues. **Generative themes** help highlight the dilemma behind many social conditions and can lead to action and change.

At The Alternate School, generative themes appear through innovative curriculum. "Gender Issues," "Great Thinkers," and "Student in Society" are three separate courses that are based on student-generated issues. These courses have been created and piloted at The Alternate School and have been approved and accepted by the Ministry of Education of Quebec as accredited secondary-leaving courses.

Student-Centred Dialogue

Creating a safe environment in the classroom for students to express their concerns about relevant issues is one of the single most important tasks for teachers practising critical pedagogy. Just as generative themes permit students to explore these issues, student-centred dialogue serves as the vehicle for this exploration. Through the development of **voice,** freedom, and **empowerment,** students engage in dialogues that transform their resistance to an acceptance that they can contribute to the teaching/learning process.

Voice, according to Weiler, is a tool that allows the teacher and students to recognize themselves as active agents of change. At The Alternate School, most classrooms have a climate of trust. Students safely discuss their cultural and personal experiences, such as rape, incest, incarceration, discrimination, and sexism. Through this discussion, teachers and students understand how the hegemonic ideology and institutional practices frame experiences, develop cultural meanings, and construct individual identities. The sharing of biographies and multiple subjectivities helps the individual to emerge as a dynamic member of the educational process. A safe atmosphere for voicing subjectivities also helps to develop consciousness.

Voice also allows the meaning of words to be validated. Since words and language do not exist as neutral tools of expression, individuals adopt and appropriate the language, making it their own. Words and language are shared and interpreted within a context. At The Alternate School, in order for teachers to converse and communicate with their students, it is imperative that they develop an understanding of students' argot. Not only does the use of argot in the classroom help teachers with youth subcultures, but it also shows students the importance of language as a contextual tool.

At The Alternate School, one particular situation points to the change that can occur when a student chooses to voice resistance. Sally, an 18-year-old female, was extremely weak in math. Her confidence was more than doubly shattered when the males in the class openly taunted her with the stereotype of "being blonde, female, and dumb." Regardless of reprimands, their behaviour changed only superficially. Each day, Sally would state that the taunts didn't bother her, since she "was used to guys bugging her." Unable to quickly change the behaviour of the group, the teacher worked on changing the behaviour of the individual instead. Talking with Sally about standing up for herself actually led to change. When she finally saw her situation as problematic, Sally decided to resist the stereotype regarding her skills. One day while struggling to solve a math problem on the board with the class snickering all around her, Sally finally stated her dissatisfaction with her male counterparts. Silence descended upon the room. She successfully finished the problem, and the class cheered. (Sally still struggles with math, but smiles since she silenced the males.)

When students are allowed to express their voice through a student-centered dialogue, they may often experience the opportunities that freedom of choice may bring. An illustration of how students exercise their freedom lies in the work experience component of the course "Student In Society." Students attend school four days a week with the fifth day serving as an accredited work-experience day. They volunteer with local businesses (i.e., offices, garages, restaurants) or community agencies (i.e., centres for the homeless, hospitals, schools, day care centres, senior citizen homes, etc.). Linking students to local communities helps on many levels. Students are

free to make the choice to engage either positively or negatively in the work placement. When students make the choice to immerse themselves in the placement, they are often offered part- or full-time jobs. Respectable employment leads to many opportunities, and students understand how choices affect their lives. They understand the constraints of their actions.

The idea of freedom is closely linked to the idea of empowerment in critical pedagogy. To empower does not imply to give power to students, but rather "to help them exercise power"(Weiler, 1988, p. 59). This orientation removes teachers from the position of authority and benevolent givers of power. Empowerment requires that teachers understand the limits and errors often involved in human judgements as well as the inconsistencies of human action.

At The Alternate School, the philosophy of placing students in situations that challenge their desire to change is witnessed in most actions. For example, it is the responsibility of the student, not the parent, the lawyer, the psychologist, or the social worker to make the initial phone call to establish an interview time. All communication is with the students; parents play a secondary role. At the start of each year, a "Parents Night" is held to introduce parents and guardians to the school and its philosophy. Following this session, parents are asked not to return until the end-of-year ceremony. All report cards are given to the student. All disciplinary measures are established with the student, regardless of their age. Any parent-teacher-student conference must be approved by the student, and consequences for actions are determined in a cooperative manner. For example, after lengthy discussions with their core teacher (significant advocate), students who have broken the law will step forward, with their core teacher present, to report the crime to both the legal authorities and their guardians. Teachers help students to analyze the situation and readjust their frame of reference so that they can make respectable, normative choices regarding their future behaviour.

Students, as a group, determine how the day will unfold. There are no bells, no structured periods for instruction, no lunch hours, and no set time to end the day. Teachers and students determine how much time to spend on each subject, based on the interest and motivation of the group as a whole. Students may eat their lunch during teaching time. Students end their school day when their lessons and work for the day are done. In some cases, teachers and students have stayed at school to complete unfinished assignments anywhere from midnight to six o'clock in the morning.

Source: Adapted from an article by Joyce Barakett and Judith Leonard, Resisting Youth Subcultures: Classroom Practice and Critical Pedagogy, *Transformations: The Journal of Curriculum Transformation 10*(2). Printed with permission, *Transformations*.

Critique of The Alternate School

In general, the Alternate School demonstrates the key elements of Freire's (1968) critical pedagogy while working with youth subcultures in the secondary school system. This is a school that does not use traditional classroom methods, such as tracking (the grouping of students according to academic abilities) or standardized textbooks. It is a school that demonstrates the worth of its troubled students not only by its philosophy and practice but also by its physical location and appearance. Housed in a shopping mall, the school is decorated (by students) with wallpaper, wicker furniture, Monet prints, plants, and includes a modern kitchen. It has created partnership with parents, the community, police, businesses, psychologists, social workers, the media, and the local universities. Students spend more time reading, thinking, and talking than taking notes and listening to lectures.

Yet, The Alternate School is not without its limitations. First, teachers and students alike enter their relationships with ingrained patterns of behaviour and learned beliefs about power. For some teachers and students, it is difficult to disavow authority. For some students, the presence of authority fuels their aggression and resistance, making it very difficult to work with them. Furthermore, teacher interests can either enable or constrain students in the classroom discourse. Teachers are critical players in influencing the climate of their classroom because they are the gatekeepers of the generative themes. In essence, it is the teachers who funnel the discourse. Sometimes, when the climate for discourse is not trustworthy, teachers fall into the trap of defending their own interests rather than exploring that of the students. It is an on-going process for teachers to release their views of authority and to encourage their students to share their values, intuition, insight, and philosophy.

Second, since The Alternate School is recognized by the Ministry of Education, the mainstream curriculum must still be covered. Students are required to write the standardized provincial examinations in June and compete for entrance into post-secondary programs. These time and curriculum constraints limit the number of generative themes that can be covered. Third, due to budget cuts, certain courses, such as art, dance, and music have fallen by the wayside. Such a restriction creates students who, as Shor explains, have "become cultural deficits dependent on the teacher as a delivery system" (1993, p. 31). Fourth, the partnership with business is tenuous, since it requires a delicate balance between accepting their financial support while diverting their philosophical input. Critical pedagogy is a call for The Alternate School to continue being critical and emancipatory rather than a functional thumbprint of the elite. But change is slow. As Shor states, "the transformation of teachers and students from authoritarian to democratic habits is a long-term project" (1993, p. 29).

We have witnessed the success of critical pedagogy at The Alternate School, both on a personal level with students and on a bureaucratic level, with the accreditation of school-generated courses. This success has also carried over to professional development at the school. Over the years, teachers have attended endless workshops, conferences, and seminars on troubled adolescents and youth subcultures. Feeling dissatisfied with the content, they embarked on a plan for their own professional training. They shadowed two youth vice detectives from the anti-gang squad of the Montreal police force on night shift. The teachers literally "walked the streets" to obtain first-hand knowledge of youth subcultures in action. In sum, the teachers recognized their needs, resisted mainstream training, and took action, putting critical pedagogy to work on themselves as well as their students.

FEMINIST PEDAGOGY

As noted in Chapter 2, the orientation of critical and feminist theory is derived from the recognition that experience and knowledge are politically charged and interrelated. Thus knowledge must be used as a practical tool for change, to alleviate oppressive social conditions, to question the ideological foundations of society, and to bring about greater equality.

Gore points out the difference between critical and feminist pedagogy as well as the differences within each. She perceives two main strands of discourse within critical pedagogy. One strand "emphasizes the articulation of a broad social and educational vision" (for example, the works of Giroux and McLaren, which aim to politicize teachers and students concerning social injustices and inequities), and the other strand (distinguished by the works of Paulo Freire and Ira Shor) focuses on "developing explicit educational practices to suit specific contexts" (Gore, 1993, p.17).

As in critical pedagogy, **feminist pedagogy** also has two strands of discourse. Unlike critical pedagogy, however, these strands are distinguished by their respective communities of writers, not by individuals. One strand emphasizes the instructional aspects of pedagogy through women's studies programs, the other emphasizes feminism(s) and theories of schools of education. The feminist pedagogy that is found in women's studies programs focuses on what constitutes feminist pedagogy, while the feminist pedagogy that is constructed in education departments (or schools of education) focuses on how gendered knowledge and experience are produced and transmitted.

Both critical and feminist pedagogy are concerned with democratizing schools and society. Feminist pedagogy, however, deals specifically with gender oppression, self-reflection, and personal experience. For the most part, the objective is to develop new criteria for what is considered to be knowledge rather than merely adding to the existing knowledge about women. The aim is also to allow for the development of women's abilities through education to increase both their influence on and their control of the representation and distribution of knowledge in academic settings and, ultimately, in society as a whole. For this, **a gender-inclusive** curriculum is essential. A gender-inclusive curriculum includes not only the writings and life experiences of women but also women's accounts and interpretations of history, as well as their analyses of the body of knowledge (produced mainly by men) that has come to be considered the appropriate content of curricula for all (Fox-Genovese, 1986).

Feminist Critique of Critical Pedagogy

Like Freirean pedagogy, feminist pedagogy strives for changes in structures of inequality. According to Shrewsbury, feminist pedagogy

> ...does not automatically preclude any technique or approach. ...It is not limited to any specific subject matter but it does include a reflexive element that increases the feminist scholarship component involved in the teaching/learning of any subject matter. It has close ties with other liberatory pedagogies, but it cannot be subsumed under other pedagogical approaches. It is transformative, but it can also be phased into a traditional teaching approach or another alternative pedagogical approach (1987, p.12).

However, Freire's educational theory does not consider inequalities based on gender. It must be expanded, therefore, to include multiple and sometimes contradictory forms of oppression. That is, theorists must acknowledge the diverse identities and subjectivities produced by different social and historical conditions (Weiler, 1991; Brady, 1994).

A number of transformative possibilities for an educational practice are reflected in the work of various feminist educational theorists. Here we wish to focus on the works of Weiler (1988, 1991) and articles in Luke and Gore (1992), studies that examine critical pedagogy from various standpoints. They critique the institutional practice of teaching, the discourse of critical pedagogy, and the educational practice resulting from this discourse. And, since critical pedagogy involves a critique and interpretation of pedagogy, feminist theorists and pedagogists challenge critical theorists and pedagogists to reexamine how their own assumptions and thoughts affect their discursive practices.

Weiler (1988), who confronts the difference between feminist and critical pedagogies and advocates "teaching for change," points to how some teachers, in their everyday work in schools, can interject feminist theory as a natural part of the teaching process through course content, questions asked, and responses to students' questions. She is concerned with how concepts are used to analyze the schooling process and how critical pedagogy can be used by teachers "teaching for change." She notes that the women in her study described their classrooms as places where consciousness and meanings were questioned, and analysis and criticisms of tests or assignments were encouraged.

However much we would like to think that there are many teachers who are generating change through their classroom practices, the reality is that two major constraints exist: educational emphasis on order and control, and institutional hierarchy. For instance, a few feminist teachers in Weiler's study question ideology, nurture resistance, and encourage change, but there are many who are caught in resistance, which causes greater domination and submission of both themselves and their students (Acker, 1988; Lewis, 1990). On the other hand, Ellsworth (1990), whose concern is with the contradictions of critical pedagogy, interprets her experience of teaching a course, "Media and Antiracist Pedagogies." An important distinction between Ellsworth and other feminist and critical theorists in education is that her study is based on personal experience. Her main objective is to analyze the discourse in studies of critical pedagogy in relation to her own experiences. She asks, Which interpretations do these discourses facilitate, which do they marginalize or silence, and whose interests do they serve?

Ellsworth's attempts to teach and practice antiracist pedagogy in the university classroom using critical pedagogy discourse proved to be ineffective. She argues that the discourse of critical pedagogy and the key assumptions, goals, and pedagogical practices that underlie it give rise to repressive myths.

Rather than pointing to how the problems she encountered in her practice of critical pedagogy could lead to reformulations of concepts in critical pedagogy, Ellsworth's essay opposes critical pedagogy. Luke, in her essay "Feminist Politics in Radical Pedagogy," also criticizes critical pedagogical discourse for being masculinist, which "...renders its emancipatory agenda for gender theoretically and practically problematic" (1992, p. 25). Thus critical pedagogy reinforces the master patriarchal narratives. Luke notes that "Theorists who do not engage substantively with feminist theory and research, of course cannot be expected to contribute to a feminist reworking of theory or politics, or to renounce the patriarchal signifier in theories and texts..." (p. 40). But Luke goes on to argue for a pedagogy that focuses on the struggle of identities and subjectivity or disclosure of the self, one which accounts for differences.

Weiler, in *Freire and a Feminist Pedagogy of Difference* (1991), supports the notion that

> ...in action, the goals of liberation or opposition to oppression have not always been easy to understand or achieve. As universal goals, these ideals do not address the specificity of people's lives; they do not directly analyze the contradictions between conflicting oppressed groups or the ways in which a single individual can experience oppression in one sphere while being privileged or oppressive in another (p.450).

Rather than dismiss critical pedagogy because it is masculinist, Weiler argues that we need to reexamine the assumptions underlying critical and liberatory classroom practices. She believes that feminist pedagogy can enhance liberatory pedagogy. For instance, in her analysis of the role and authority of the teacher she notes that "there is an institutionally imposed authority of the teacher" (p. 460). But women asserting this authority in their classroom practices must also strive to empower students by having them question and analyze their own experience and recognize their own power. In other words, feminist pedagogy can address the contradictions between the goals of feminism and the hierarchies of power and knowledge in school settings. She notes that

> Recognizing the standpoint of subjects as shaped by their experience of class, race, gender, or other socially defined identities has powerful implications for pedagogy, in that it emphasizes the need to make conscious the subject positions not only of students but of teachers as well (p.470).

What is missing in the theoretical writings of many of the critical and feminist pedagogists is a clearly articulated vision of how their ideas translate into actual practice, especially in school settings where established ways of doing things are thoroughly entrenched. Not only would the prescriptions for change insert themselves in the system, but, in so doing, cause a reaction, at once institutional and individual. As we saw earlier, the norms of the teaching profession promote harmony and thus operate to support the status quo. The challenge, then, is to effect change without bringing about such counterresistance that the status quo is reinforced.

Weiler and others (Giroux, 1989) suggest that we develop a pedagogy *of difference, for difference*. Such a pedagogy sheds light on the conflicting ideologies and social experiences of students' lives, allowing students and their teachers to understand the practices that take place in their political, cultural, and social milieux.

SUMMARY/CONCLUSIONS

Briefly then, critical theorists and pedagogists provide insights for studying the relationship between school and society. They have developed a dialectical framework to understand what mediates or exists between institutions and activities of everyday life. Freire, in particular, developed a conceptual framework in which the connection between theory and practice illuminated how vested interests underlie knowledge formation itself. Thus Freire helped us to see how knowledge has political as well as practical content. When competing interests vie for the legitimacy of particular forms of knowledge those in positions of power claim that their knowledge has been substantiated scientifically and is, therefore, more valid than the other forms of knowledge. In the field of education, one sees this kind of competition between those who adhere to a quantitative approach to research and those who prefer a qualitative approach. Since the quantitative approach has been borrowed from the so-called "hard sciences," the voices of its advocates tend to be the ones that are heard.

Critical educational theorists and pedagogists argue that society is both exploitative and oppressive, but that it can also be changed. They emphasize individual empowerment, social transformation, and the need to develop critical consciousness in students.

The study "Resisting Youth Subcultures: Classroom Practice and Critical Pedagogy" illustrates how teachers and school administrators can respect the consciousness, concerns, and culture of their students by creating a pedagogical setting in which students can express their problems and understanding of their social environment. When teachers reflect on their own assumptions about students' behaviours they create an environment where dialogue can occur.

Feminist educational theorists and feminist pedagogists have both been concerned with the production and reproduction of gender inequity under a system of patriarchy. They are critical of the role of schools in reproducing class differences and gender stereotypes. They focus on ways in which patriarchal assumptions define both school practices and research in education, ways in which schools and curricula have reproduced racist ideology and assumptions, and the openings that exist for teachers to use students' own cultural worlds as the source for oppositional pedagogy. They build on earlier critical educational studies, in particular, the work of Paulo Freire.

For its recognition of the position of the powerless in society, Freire's work is without parallel. Freire illuminates what is needed to break through the practices which portray a false reality. Freire had the courage to add these insights to the tapestry of what we consider knowledge.

Finally, both critical and feminist pedagogists share an underlying concern with the relationship between the individual subject and an oppressive social structure. Both demonstrate the tensions between the production and reproduction of theoretical approaches; and both emphasize that social structures and knowledge are socially constructed and, therefore, open to resistance and change.

In the following chapter, we focus on the informal socializing features of the school, and how these affect students' academic performance. In addition, Chapter 5 examines the influence of peer groups and popular culture on the ability of the school to perform its socialization function.

KEY TERMS

conscientization	feminist pedagogy	praxis
critical pedagogy	gender-inclusive	resistance
culture of silence	curriculum	theory of liberation
dialogue	generative themes	voice
empowerment	pedagogy	

DISCUSSION QUESTIONS

1. Discuss and reflect upon the differences between critical and feminist pedagogy.
2. Which do you think can best address the problems of social inequality, feminist or critical pedagogy?
3. Discuss what is meant by the politics of education and cultural politics.

RECOMMENDED READINGS/REFERENCES

Acker, S. (1988). Teachers, gender and resistance. *British Journal of Sociology of Education*, *9*, pp. 307–322.

Aikenhead, G. S. (1990). Scientific/technological literacy, critical reasoning, and classroom practice. In S. P Norris, & L. M. Phillips (Eds.), *Foundations of literacy policy in Canada* (pp.127–146). Calgary: Detselig.

Aronowitz, S., & Giroux, H. (1993). *Education still under siege.* London: Bergin and Garvey.

Barakett, J., & Leonard, J. (1999). Resisting youth subcultures: Classroom practice and critical pedagogy. *Transformations: The Journal of Curriculum Transformation*, *10*(2).

Bibby, R., & Posterski, D. (1992). *Teen trends: A nation in motion.* Toronto: Stoddart.

Brady, J. (1994). Critical literacy, feminism, and politics of representation. In C. Lankshear, & P. McLaren (Eds.), *Politics of liberation: Paths from Freire* (pp. 142–153). New York: Routledge.

Carrasco, R. L. (1981). Expanded awareness of student performance: A case study in applied ethnographic monitoring in a bilingual classroom. In H. Trueba, G. P. Guthrie, & K. Au Hu-Pei. (Eds.), *Culture and the bilingual classroom* (pp. 153–177). Rowley: Newbury House Publishers.

Cleghorn, A., & Genesee, F. (1984). Languages in contact: An ethnographic study of interaction in an immersion school. *TESOL Quarterly, 18*(4), 595–625.

Diamond, I., & Quinby, L. (Eds.). (1988). *Feminisms and Foucault: Reflections on resistance.* Boston: Northwestern University Press.

Ellsworth, E. (1990). Why doesn't this feel empowering? Working through repressive myths and critical pedagogy. In C. Luke, & J. Gore (Eds.), *Feminisms and critical pedagogies.* New York: Routledge.

Fox-Genovese, E. (1986). Gender, race, class, canon. *Salmagundi: A Quarterly of the Humanities & Social Sciences, 72,* 131–143.

Freire, P. (1968). *Pedagogy of the oppressed.* New York: Seabury Press.

Freire, P. (1973). *Education for critical consciousness.* New York: Seabury Press.

Freire, P. (1985). *The politics of education: Culture, power and liberation.* Boston: Bergin and Garvey.

Fuller, B., & Snyder, C. W. (1991). Vocal teachers, silent pupils: Life in Botswana classrooms. *Comparative Education review, 35*(2), 274–294.

Giroux, H. (1983). *Theory and resistance in education.* Massachusetts: Bergin and Garvey.

Giroux, H. (1989). Schooling as a form of cultural politics: Towards a pedagogy of and for difference. In H. Giroux & P. McLaren (Eds.), *Critical pedagogy, the state and cultural struggle* (pp. 125–151). New York: State University of New York Press.

Giroux, H. (1996). *Fugitive Cultures: Race, violence and youths.* England: Routledge.

Giroux, H., & McLaren, P. (1989). *Critical pedagogy, the state and cultural struggle.* Albany: State University of New York Press.

Giroux, H., & McLaren, P. (1994). *Between borders.* New York:Routledge.

Gore, J. (1992). Feminist politics in radical pedagogy. In C. Luke, & J. Gore (Eds.), *Feminisms and critical pedagogies* (pp. 25–53). New York: Routledge.

Gore, J. (1993). *The struggle for pedagogies.* New York: Routledge.

Lewis, M. (1992). Interrupting patriarchy: Politics, resistance and transformation in the feminist classroom. In C. Luke, & J.Gore (Eds.) *Feminisms and critical pedagogies* (pp. 167–191). New York: Routledge.

Luke, C., & Gore, J. (1992). *Feminisims and critical pedagogies.* New York: Routledge.

McLaren, P. (1998). *Life in schools: An introduction to critical pedagogy in the foundations of education (3rd. ed.).* Don Mills: Langerman.

McLaren, P,. & Lankshear, C. (Eds.). (1994). *Politics of liberation: Paths from Freire.* New York:Routledge.

McLaren, P., & Leonard, P. (1993).(Eds.). *Paulo Freire: A critical encounter.* New York: Routledge.

Norris, S. P., & Phillips, L. M. (1990). *Foundations of literacy policy in Canada.* Calgary, AB: Detselig.

Shor, I. (1988). *Freire for the* classroom: *A sourcebook for liberatory teaching.* Portsmouth: Bayton/Cook.

Shor, I. (1992). *Empowering education: Critical teaching for social change.* Chicago: University of Chicago Press.

Shor, I. (1993). Education is politics: Paulo Freire's critical pedagogy. In P. McLaren, & P. Leonard (Eds.), *Paulo Freire: A critical encounter* (pp. 25–35). New York: Routledge.

Short, J. (1968). *Gang Delinquency and Delinquent Subcultures.* New York: Harper and Row.

Shrewsbury, C. M. (1987). What is feminist pedagogy?, *Women's Studies Quarterly, 15* (3–4), pp. 6–14.

Simon, R. (1987, April). Empowerment as a pedagogy of possibility. *Language Arts, 64*(4), 370–382.

Trueba, H., Guthrie, G. P., & Au Hu-Pei, K. (1981). *Culture and the bilingual classroom.* Rowley: Newbury House Publishers.

Weber, M. (1947). *The theory of social and economic organization.* New York: The Free Press.

Weiler, K. (1988). *Women teaching for change: Gender, class and power.* Boston: Bergin and Garvey.

Weiler, K. (1991). Freire and a feminist pedagogy of difference, *Harvard Educational Review, 16* (4), pp. 449–475.

Weiler, K., & Mitchell, C. (1992). *What schools can do: Critical pedagogy and practices.* New York: State University of New York Press.

Willis, P. (1977). *Learning to labour.* New York: Columbia University Press.

THE SCHOOL AS AN INFORMAL SYSTEM OF SOCIALIZATION

Chapter Objectives

This chapter focuses on the role of the school in the process of socialization. It compares the socialization that takes place within the family with the socialization that takes place in the school. From here, we explain how the two domains of socialization come together in the classroom, primarily through the expectations that teachers develop toward students. The chapter demonstrates how teachers' expectations intersect with organizational features of the school and with classroom management considerations, which in turn affect the child's academic potential as well as her or his identity. We also discuss how teachers' expectations are based on schemes of interpretations of students' behaviours. Thus we see in this chapter how subtly these processes produce and reproduce an achievement history at both the individual and the group level, with further ramifications for patterns of inequality in society at large.

The chapter begins with a brief discussion of various theories of the socialization process as it occurs within the family. It then moves on to discuss socialization within the school and the classroom, including a mention of the role of the school in both moral and political socialization. Finally, we look at the socializing influence of peer groups, the hidden curriculum, the media, and popular culture on the lives and education of young people today.

THEORIES OF SOCIALIZATION

Socialization refers to the complex, life-long learning process through which individuals develop a sense of self and acquire the knowledge, skills, values, norms, and dispositions required to fulfill social roles. Stated differently, socialization refers to the process through which the individual takes on the ways of thinking, seeing, believing, and behaving that prevail in the society that he or she was born into. Within a complex society, social roles and obligations vary; they reflect differences in social class, ethnicity, race, and gender as well as the constant changes within the society. There are several agents of socialization—family, school, peer groups, and the media.

Primary socialization occurs in the micro world of the family, which is a primary group. It involves the development of language and individual identity as well as identity relating to the particular ethnic or religious subgroup that the family may belong to. It involves learning cognitive skills and self control as well as the internalization of moral standards. It also involves the development of appropriate attitudes and behaviours for social interactions, and an understanding of social roles. Gender identity and an understanding of masculinity and femininity are also learned during primary socialization. Primary socialization is most influential in the years before a child goes to school; however, the influence of the family persists after that, along with influence of the school. The school is the main agent of secondary socialization.

Originally, the concept of socialization was used to refer to a process of eliminating children's inherent unruly behaviours. Over time, as educators and psychologists learned more about childhood and child development, socialization came to be seen as a process of **internalization** in which the individual incorporates the appropriate social norms, roles, and values into their own mind.

The functionalist view of socialization perceives the individual as reacting and responding to people and situations in her or his world according to sets of more or less structured situational responses. This perspective is perhaps most clearly stated by Parsons (1967), who viewed the school classroom as a system that socializes and allocates individuals on the basis of the criteria assigned to it by the larger society. Differentiation of status occurs on the basis of achievement not ascription. He summarizes his views in the following way:

> The essential point...seems to be that the elementary school, regarded in the light of its socialization function, is an agency which differentiates the school class broadly along a single continuum of achievement, the content of which is relative excellence in living up to the expectations imposed by the teacher as an agent of the adult society. The criteria of this achievement are, generally speaking, differentiated into the cognitive or technical component and the moral or "social" component (p. 653).

Thus social reality is viewed as objective, external to and independent of the individual. Socialized people know what is expected of them because they are introduced to and socialized into a culturally specific but generally shared system of symbols, meanings, and values. Socialization is considered necessary to ensure the stability and functioning of the social system.

There are a number of other theoretical perspectives used to explore and explain the socialization process. Freud's psychoanalytic theory, for instance, relies heavily on biological factors to explain the development of identity, personality, and behaviour. Freud believed that the mind's irrational and subconscious features are at the base of human behaviour and that early childhood experiences in the family determine adult socialization. He stated that the child is born with an **id** but must progress through developmental changes in order to develop an **ego** and a **superego**. The id refers to the individual's biological or unconscious instincts that seek immediate gratification. The ego controls and checks the id. It deals with the world in terms of what is possible, providing limits and direction to the id. The demand on the id and the ego includes recognizing the limits imposed on them by the superego. The superego, which is the individual's conscience, strives to regulate behaviour within acceptable societal norms.

Piaget, who is best known for developing the **cognitive perspective,** emphasizes the development of perceptions and thought processes. Behavioural standards are the result of the child's identification with her or his parents, who have communicated society's rules through a system of reward, punishment, and example (Mackie, 1994). Piaget explains children's behaviour in terms of their mental efforts to organize their social environment. Similar to Freud, Piaget explains human behaviour as the collaboration of biological and environmental factors. At the centre of Piaget's theory is the development of moral thought. Children are perceived as active learners, attempting to develop a sense of right and wrong. Changes to the child's thought processes are demonstrated through the development of two levels of morality. *Moral realism,* which is generally attained between the ages of four and seven, judges misbehaviour in terms of the consequences of the act, and *moral autonomy,* generally achieved by the ages of seven to nine, concerns itself with the reasons for misbehaving. The moral realists are not concerned with extenuating circumstances or the intentions of the one misbehaving. They believe that rules are sacred and deviations should not be tolerated. On the other hand, moral autonomists view rules as "arbitrary social conventions" that could be adapted to particular situations. For Piaget, the development of morality is made possible through the maturation of cognitive ability, which evolves from the interaction between genetic capacities and social experiences (Mackie, 1994).

In contrast to Freud's and Piaget's theories, the **social learning theory** focuses exclusively on the environmental factors surrounding the child. One principle of this theoretical approach is the notion of reinforcement and how it shapes behaviour to conform with the expectations of socialization agents such as parents and teachers. The child is perceived as a passive learner influenced by the rewards and punishment for appropriate and inappropriate behaviours. This theory also states that children learn vicariously by observing and imitating the behaviour, beliefs, and norms held by those closest to them. From this stance, observational learning also appears to be mainly responsible for the acquisition of language. Children imitate language and learn the meaning of words in the same way they learn other forms of behaviour.

The theoretical perspectives that we emphasize to explain the process of socialization are symbolic interaction, phenomenology, and interpretive sociology. Symbolic interaction

(Mead, 1934) stresses the ongoing process of interpreting and defining actions in order to construct meanings for various situations. Phenomenologists and interpretive sociologists (Schutz, 1973) are concerned with the knowledge and assumptions that individuals need to make sense of and assign meaning to the world.

Mead's Theory

Mead explains that socialization of individuals occurs through the development of a self, which depends on language and social interation. As noted in Chapter 2, Mead's concept of *self* includes the *me,* which represents internalized societal attitudes and expectations, and the *I,* which represents the spontaneity and individuality of the person. He defined the self as that which is an object to oneself. That is, the self is reflexive. The individual becomes an object to herself or himself by taking into account the attitude of **significant others,** those with whom he or she has the most frequent and consistent interaction. These people are primary socialization agents. In this reflexive process, the individual notes, selects, and determines the responses and actions he or she will take. Thus the individual is not merely reacting but is an active agent interpreting, selecting, and then acting.

The ability to look objectively at oneself depends on the acquisition of language. The acquisition of language and the development of a self require role-taking and role-playing. The child is able to play the role of the other by imitating the behaviour of the significant other, but the child does not understand this behaviour. Role-playing involves the child playing at being a mother, father, teacher, or other adult. That is, the child *plays* at taking different roles and acts out the same responses that these roles call out in others. This is different from role-taking, where the child is not merely imitating the behaviours of others, but understands the responsibilities attached to the role.

Eventually, the child is able to take the role of the **generalized other,** which consists of the attitudes of the community or society as a whole. At this point, the child has learned to compare and hold different judgments or impressions. The child has learnt the *rules of the game.*

The self develops as a result of social interaction with others, who provide meaning of the self through their responses. Cooley (1956) called this the looking-glass self. Responses, in other words, are taken as representations of what the self must be. Through language, the individual has the ability for symbolic representation and observes the world through a defining and labeling process. What the individual takes into account in this process depends on the existing needs, feelings, purpose, expectations, and rules of the group.

The above theoretical concepts emphasize that situations are created, sustained, and "made to happen" by individuals; that is, they may be said to be **socially constructed.** Children do not behave in certain ways due simply to the internalization of norms, rather they actively construct situations by negotiating with themselves and others the norms and meanings they will use in a particular situation. There is a negotiated character to norms, and norms are interpreted in relation to interests. These interpretations are guided by the socialization process. From this perspective, the child's own thoughts and evaluations are not based simply on instinct or the objective reality of the situation.

Family background, which includes social class, ethnicity, language, gender, cultural practices, and religion, influences the primary socialization process. As indicated above, when the child enters the school system the **secondary socialization** process begins. Secondary socialization refers to the social learning that occurs in institutions such as schools. The extent of socialization in the school depends on the child's family background. Teachers and peers join family members as authorities as well as significant others. In this context, a teacher may affect the student in a manner that is comparable to a parent or other close relative. While friends and other adults, such as athletic coaches, may also become significant others, it is important to point out that the significance lies more in the mind and interpretations of the child than in the shared and conscious part of the relationship itself. A more conscious relationship is referred to as **mentoring.**

Schutz's Theory

Following Mead's tradition, Alfred Schutz further explains what occurs in the social interaction process. He emphasized the importance of examining the interpretive principles and methods that individuals use to make sense of a situation. He stresses that to understand social interaction we must uncover or make explicit the hidden facts of the interaction process. For him this means we must understand how individuals act in the context of an intersubjective reality. **Intersubjectivity** refers to the knowledge we have accumulated through our experiences, including the knowledge about others that has been transmitted to us by parents and teachers. Schutz refers to this knowledge as commonsense knowledge, since it is knowledge that individuals have at hand, which they can draw on for the practical purpose of defining an object, situation, or event. This knowledge serves as a scheme of interpretation for the individual's past and current experiences.

Schutz then goes on to note that commonsense knowledge or schemes of interpretation consist of institutionalized beliefs or constructs of typifications (social types) that help individuals understand the actions of others in similar situations. By taking the subjective position, Schutz attempts to interpret the larger contexts of interactional situations. That is, he tries to explain how individuals construct social types by drawing on larger social contexts and then behave on the basis of them. For him, the self, language, and interpretations of objects and situations emerge through the typification process (copying of social types), rather than through the internalization of Mead's generalized other (Schutz, 1973).

TEACHER EXPECTATIONS

Schools teach selected ideals, values, skills, and kinds of knowledge that have been deemed important. To understand how the educational process affects an individual's academic performance as well as his or her status position we must analyze interaction patterns in the school setting. Inequality in educational settings, or in society in general, is not merely a question of differing values, social positions, or social and cultural backgrounds. To more clearly understand how social inequality is perpetuated in the classroom, we will examine how teachers use unquestioned, commonsense knowledge to interpret and respond to their pupils' behaviours.

Teacher Typifications of Pupils

Teachers' expectations of students have been internalized through teacher education programs and through their own experiences with teachers. Student teachers are taught how to evaluate, classify, and place pupils into high-, middle-,or low-ability groups. They are taught that this is a good way to dovetail instruction to the learners' needs, and to facilitate the management of their classes. Sometimes this process results in two or more streams and separate classes at the same grade level; other times it results in the formation of different ability groups within a single class. This is referred to as **tracking**. Tracking is supported through the use of standardized tests, the results of which are believed to be objective and unbiased. As a student accumulates an achievement record, he or she will come to think of himself or herself in terms of the grade or value that he or she is accustomed to receiving. Thus a child who is consistently placed in the lower level reading group may come to think of himself or herself as slow. Even though the initial criteria for such a placement may have been faulty the child internalizes the effects of the placement. Tracking is important because the social meanings attached to these groupings find their equivalence in the social groups of society at large.

Although there is much discussion among teachers about the importance of encouraging children who are having difficulties to perform better in school, there are important classroom management considerations that militate against this actually occurring. For example, during the first week of school, children in Grade 1(most of whom may not be able to read at all) may be placed into high-, medium- or low-level reading groups, simply to give the class a structure, making it easier for the teacher to manage in the difficult early days of the school year. Once the groups are formed, however, the boundaries tend to become rigid. Children quickly understand that they have been placed in the "smart" group or the "slow" group and may report the fact to parents. If, for example, the teacher should then decide that a child has mistakenly been placed in the high-level reading group, the teacher will then have to find a satisfactory explanation for what may seem like a demotion to the child and his or her parents. Teachers sometimes use demotions as threats for behaviour management purposes, so it is not difficult to see that the social meaning attached to ability-group placement can be quite complex. In addition, it is easier to manage a class if the size and composition of the groups remain fairly constant. To move one or more children up and out of the low-level group may result in an unmanageable middle-level group, necessitating the movement of another child from the middle-level group to the high-level group, even if the demands at that level are seen as too difficult. Once formed, ability groups tend to remain as they are, contributing (rightly or wrongly) over time to the child's definition of his or her own ability and sense of self.

Indeed, one of the teacher's major dilemmas is how to go about assessing the pupil. Hargreaves et al. (1975) state that over time teachers develop elaborate **typifications** of individual pupils. These typifications become part of teachers' commonsense knowledge about students in the classroom. The teacher speculates on the sort of character the pupil has. Generally, the constructs used to assess a student's character are appearance, language ability, conformity to discipline, acceptance of their academic role, general likableness, and relations with peers. The teacher may also have knowledge of the pupil's social class background and records from previous schooling as well as information from informal discussions with other teachers. As the teacher accumulates more information about the student, and behaviours and interactions are repeated over time, this knowledge becomes "evidence" to confirm her or his impressions.

As Figure 5–1 shows, standards that are operative in the social organization of the teacher's daily activities are essentially situational and practical. From the teacher's stance, reasons for typifying and categorizing students are justified if they permit a measure of order, or if they follow the organization's logic. They are developed out of a practical necessity to deal with classroom activities, that is, practical circumstances and interests. Thus, ability grouping is not only the consequence of teacher expectations, dominant ideologies, and educational structures, but it is also a function of organizing routine classroom activities. Teachers are concerned with interpreting, defining, and managing their pupils' classroom behaviours for the practical purpose of teaching prescribed content to a variety of students.

It is true that teachers are largely bound by the world they live in and by their knowledge of that world. Differentiating their student population helps them to define the characteristics and expectations of performance. Since intelligence and competence are highly valued in our society, teachers are obviously concerned with identifying these characteristics among their students. Typifying, comparing, and classifying student ability helps teachers operate with minimal conflict in an otherwise bureaucratic organization.

Apple (1979) states that the differentiation of students through grading also helps to establish the occupational division of labour. The procedures that stratify students, culturally and economically through the application of values and categories, are part of the larger political and economic context within which schools are located. It is, however, important to examine these commonsense social principles and values. As Apple notes,

> ...certain types of cultural capital—types of performance, knowledge, dispositions, achievements, and propensities—are not necessarily good in and of themselves. They are often historically and ideologically "conditioned." The categories that we employ to think through what we are doing with students, their and our success and failure, are involved in a process

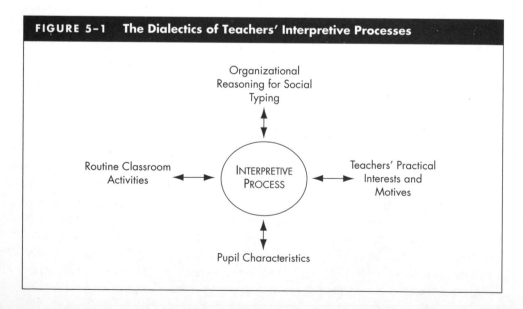

FIGURE 5–1   The Dialectics of Teachers' Interpretive Processes

Organizational Reasoning for Social Typing

Routine Classroom Activities ← → INTERPRETIVE PROCESS ← → Teachers' Practical Interests and Motives

Pupil Characteristics

of social valuing. The guiding principles that we use to plan, order, and evaluate our activity —conceptions of achievement, of success and failure, of good and bad students—are *social and economic* constructs...the very ways we talk about students provide excellent instances of the mechanisms through which dominant ideologies operate (p.130).

The concept of purpose is important in the analysis of how social inequality is perpetuated in the classroom. First, purposes can operate as masked reasons for actions. That is, some teachers are not reflexive about their purposes or interests, nor about the actions they take based on these. Teachers may not be aware that their purposes produce political, moral, and social consequences. Second, teachers' purposes generate general interests. For instance, actions are rationalized to accomplish specific tasks, but, at the same time, these serve general social interests. Finally, the concept helps us understand how teachers inadvertently reproduce existing structures.

The above educational practices perform a dual role in serving the dominant ideology by using purposeful definitions of the situation and by serving the interests of those who already possess economic and cultural capital. These practices are also linked to our conceptual understanding of education, and form part of a larger **taken-for-granted perspective** that dominates education. If we are to question teachers' management procedures, then we must also raise questions about how hegemony affects categorization. That is, the ways that classrooms are organized and students are categorized both stem from the dominant culture via the teacher's taken-for granted knowledge.

Phenomenologists and interpretive sociologists argue that our taken-for-granted perspectives and commonsense assumptions should be examined when analyzing how the schooling process affects educational and social inequality. The ideologies, structures, and attitudes experienced by students influence their attitudes toward their schooling process, their teachers, and themselves. These attitudes dictate student behaviours and beliefs about themselves and their world, and influence their decisions about their future. Student perceptions of self are essentially influenced by typifications, which teachers draw on for the purpose of classroom organization. Indeed, many teachers unknowingly participate in determining students' educational achievements and future positions in the social structure.

MORAL AND POLITICAL SOCIALIZATION

The French sociologist Emile Durkeim also considers that schooling passes on a society's normative system, including the organization of injustice and inequality. As agents of **moral socialization,** schools instill an idealized version of society's values. Further, the knowledge and values passed on by the school become internalized as part of the individual's commonsense understandings of the world (Durkheim, 1961). **Political socialization** refers to the role that the school plays in inculcating the values and norms that support the prevailing structure of society, including the dominant political ideology (Mifflen and Mifflen, 1982).

A historical look at the development of education in Canada will quickly indicate how thoroughly (and how early) both moral and political considerations were deemed to be the proper concerns of the educational system. With Anglicans, Presbyterians, and Roman

Catholics all vying for control, schooling was a key player in, and agent of, political socialization. According to Lazerson, as quoted by Mifflen and Mifflen (1982),

> The content of that socialization included a commitment to a Christianity that could accommodate most Protestants, to Canadians as loyal subjects of the Queen, and to social class harmony within an hierarchically ordered society (p. 20).

What is not so obvious today is how deeply influenced the system in Canada was by the British class model, which upheld one system for the elite and another for the working class. The elite system provided nearly automatic access to higher education and to leadership positions as well as careers in the professions, while children from the working class were provided with the essentials of reading and writing, but little, if any, instruction that could eventually lead to questioning the status quo. Thus, as suggested in Chapter 1, schooling was about maintaining the power structure and social status quo through social control. Although this system has supposedly disappeared with the expansion of near-universal access to post-secondary education, as indicated earlier, the most powerful positions in Canadian society are still occupied mostly by English-speaking people of Anglo-Saxon origin. As educators, we must ask what the present-day mechanisms are for this continued occurrence.

Earlier we spoke about the role of the family in the development of personal and subgroup identity. Here we suggest that it is through the school, as well as through the media, that a sense of national identity may be formed. In Canada, this sometimes takes the form of regional rather than national allegiance (at least until later on in an individual's higher education), possibly because of the Canadian tendency to believe in the value and promotion of **pluralism**. Thus, we see people from British Columbia and Alberta identifying themselves as *Westerners;* people from Ontario, *central Canadians;* French-speaking people from Quebec, *Québécois;* and people from the eastern provinces, *Maritimers.* That this description of regional affiliations and identities does not strike us as particularly threatening or unusual is testimony to the fact that we have come to see the way our society is organized as "normal." Canada is not the **melting pot** that the United States is generally accepted to be. Still, Canadian schools do appear to succeed in helping children from immigrant families become bicultural, at least through the second generation, and often well beyond that. While this may be viewed as a type of partial assimilation, a more accurate term may be integration.

THE HIDDEN CURRICULUM

The fundamental patterns in any society are held together by tacit ideological assumptions. In schools, some rules are not overt, but they serve to organize and legitimate the activities of teachers and students. Much of what the school teaches and the students learn does not appear in the formal curriculum. Successful school performance requires that the student learn what are considered important and useful skills and knowledge. But students must also have the skills to uncover the hidden rules and expectations that affect their dispositions, identities, and personalities. For example, schools emphasize conformity, deferred gratification, achievement, competitiveness, and obedience to authority. Students must understand the social and other dimensions of this hidden curriculum. The hidden curriculum refers to the tacit teaching of norms, values, and dispositions that occurs through students' participation in social experiences in routine school activities.

Functionalist writers such as Jackson (1968) and Dreeben (1968) show that the hidden curriculum is part of the regular features of the informal schooling process. They argue that, while the explicit goals of the school, which are reflected in the school curriculum, are an important part of the socialization process, students' social experiences in educational settings are also crucial factors to consider when analyzing the learning process. There are important lessons derived from the hidden curriculum that appear not to be related to the acquisition of knowledge, but, nevertheless, contribute to the student's development of an identity and personality.

Another view of the hidden curriculum is presented by Apple and Smith (1991), who point to the importance of textbooks that teach culture. They note that, "...texts are not simply "delivery" systems of "facts." They are at once the results of political, economic, and cultural activities, battles, and compromises" (p. 1). Apple and Smith stress that texts reflect the interests of those who write them, but also that texts are published in the context of "market, resources, and power." For instance, if history, sociology, or political science courses do not use texts that address how government policies eliminated traditional aboriginal cultures, how certain policies are biased against some immigrant groups, or how women have been excluded from positions of power, then students do not learn about or develop an understanding of the experiences of different people. The point is that the school's formal curriculum cannot be seen as transmitting neutral knowledge. The knowledge transmitted depends on what is included in texts as much as what is excluded from them.

Likewise, there is not only one interpretive procedure used to understand the text. Apple and Smith state, "From all we have said ...it should be clear that we oppose the idea that there can be one textual authority, one definitive set of "facts" divorced from their context of power relations" (p. 15). Finally, they argue that, as teachers, we must create the conditions necessary to enable individuals to participate in creating and, perhaps, changing meanings and values.

The Peer Group and Popular Culture

At this point we would like to turn to a discussion of peer groups and popular culture and their effects on student learning. Besides learning role models from the significant and generalized other, students are also influenced by their peer group, especially during adolescence when individuals begin to explore various possible identities and affiliations. These affiliations and the relationships that develop from them are part of the informal process of schooling, since they largely occur within the school or in association with school-related activities and may have a significant effect on students' attitudes, beliefs, and behaviour.

Many sociologists have argued that peer group values and behaviours may be more important in students' behaviours than school or parental values (Coleman, 1961; Clark & Trow, 1966; Ballantine, 1983). Adolescents develop relationships that often lead to the development of youth or student subcultures. These subcultures constitute participation in sets of norms and values that play an important role in controlling the behaviour of peer group members. For example, for boys, popularity among peers may depend on athletic skills; for girls, it may depend on appearance or personality. Thus, the student subculture may be at odds with teachers' expectations and with what schools are trying to do. We need only witness conformity in dress, gestures, language and slang to understand what is deemed acceptable among students in any particular school. Indeed, fads and crazes are important aspects of student subculture: They hold the group together. All of these aspects set the student world apart from the adult world.

Thus the norms and values of the schools and the larger society, with teachers representing the culture of the dominant group, distance the students from their teachers. Popular culture, as reflected in TV shows, films, magazines, and technological artefacts, such as Nintendo games and the Internet, which students and youth groups draw on for their general entertainment, represents another dimension that contributes to this distance between teachers and students and may affect school performance.

Students bring their knowledge of popular culture to the classroom, but this is commonly considered to be a less significant aspect of the socialization process than, say, the transmission of cultural capital (language, codes, and values of the dominant culture). The importance of popular culture, however, in shaping students', teachers', administrators', and others' view of themselves, and, subsequently, their views of different forms of pedagogy, should not be underestimateed. Students and teachers alike appropriate popular culture and incorporate this culture into their educational experiences.

Although schooling, classroom pedagogy, and popular culture do not appear to be related, Giroux and Simon (1989) state that popular culture is part of the student's everyday social life and, therefore, part of the cultural politics of the school:

> ...it is precisely in the relationship between pedagogy and popular culture that the important understanding arises of making the pedagogical more political and the political more pedagogical. Popular culture and pedagogy represent important terrains of cultural struggle which offer both subversive discourse and important theoretical elements through which it becomes possible to rethink schooling as a viable and important form of cultural politics (p. 238).

Teachers, then, must become aware of how popular culture can and does affect their pedagogical practices. Students appropriate popular culture and incorporate this culture into their educational experiences. It gives authority to their voices and experiences. Thus, it is appropriate to examine how popular culture affects the informal process of schooling. Indeed, Aronowitz and Giroux (1985) speak to the issue of mass culture and critical pedagogy by stating the following about writing:

> If writing is to become part of the critical process, deconstruction of mass culture is the first priority. We mean that writing could consist in the first place in analysis of TV shows, critical interrogation of popular music, and close scrutiny of film genres that approximate mass culture, such as disaster films, and adventures. In other words, the job of the teacher is to legitimate mass audience culture in order to criticize and transcend it, or to discover whether genuine expressive forms are repressed within it (p. 52).

Briefly, the important point is that knowledge cannot be perceived as a "neutral artefact," learned through either the formal or the informal curriculum. We must ask whose culture is being transmitted and in whose interest. Are there certain social subgroups that are related to particular knowledge and power? The debate on the formal curriculum and subject matter for appropriate schooling outcomes should shift to include the significance of texts, peer groups, youth and student subcultures, and popular culture on the informal socialization process of schooling and pedagogical practices.

TEACHER EDUCATION

We have already discussed the two main debates in teacher education programs as well as some approaches to thinking about teaching in Chapter 3 (Models of Teacher Education: Some Canadian Trends). What is left to discuss is the importance of teacher education when addressing educational and social inequality generated through the hidden curriculum.

According to Tom (1987,1995) and Liston and Zeichner (1987), pedagogical practices within teacher education programs have been influenced by dominant ideological discourses. We believe that, although many researchers argue for or against particular pedagogical practices, teacher education programs essentially fail at educational reform because the programs focus almost exclusively on technical forms of knowledge (Beyer, 1987; Smyth, 1989; Sheehan & Fullan, 1995). Similarly, the teacher's role is presumed to be one that transforms knowledge in a noncritical manner. Efficiency, classroom management and control, and getting something effectively taught, are of primary concern to many teachers. Education of this kind tends to depoliticize rather than politicize both educators and students. In particular, it disempowers rather than empowers learners, and it does not demystify hegemonic, controlling ideologies.

Fortunately, alternative discourses to traditional pedagogical approaches have gained some attention within teacher education programs. Some education reformers suggest that teacher education should prepare student teachers to question taken-for-granted practices, which are considered politically neutral.

Furthermore, as we have noted throughout this text, critical and feminist theory and pedagogy can contribute to teacher education generally, and to teaching methods courses. (Methods courses have generally emphasized the development of skills, such as planning lessons and disciplining students.) If we adopt these comparative/critical/feminist perspectives we will more easily foster a questioning attitude toward teaching, learning, knowledge, formal and hidden curricula, and towards the relationship between school and society.

Aronowitz and Giroux (1985) argue that teacher education must contribute to the development of a schooling process that works in the interests of a democratic society by viewing teacher education as a form of cultural politics. Such a program would include the study of various themes, such as language, history, culture, and power. Giroux (1989) notes,

> ...it is important that educators come to understand theoretically how difference is constructed through various representations and practices that name, legitimate, marginalize, and exclude the cultural capital and voices of various groups (p.142).

It is only through an understanding of how these can be challenged and transformed that teachers can develop a pedagogy *for* difference, one which addresses how differences are constructed in the curriculum, student voices, and conflicting ideologies. These are only some of the issues to be engaged in this approach.

This is a recent reform movement in teacher education training, which Liston and Zeichner (1991) refer to as the social-reconstructionist tradition. This tradition aims at preparing future teachers for a diverse student population. Reforms in teacher training programs must be developed to lead to critical consciousness, and to create a more democratic and just society. They argue, however, that criticism of the social-reconstructionist approach has pointed to its marginal status and is merely "an academic discussion that has had very little influence outside its own inner circle" (p.34). Furthermore, the authors note that studies show that many universities do not support social-reconstructionist-oriented reforms because they do not want to alienate those students who support the status quo in the schooling process. And, perhaps, universities do not want to risk opposing the existing institutional and societal structures (p.155).

Liston and Zeichner further note that "...most accounts of teachers' practical knowledge seem to give little emphasis to...cultural, social or political [experiences]" (p.67). However, the authors believe the social-reconstructionist tradition can contribute to the development of teacher education programs that would emphasize the notion of teachers reflecting on their social and political beliefs and challenge the reality of classroom practices. That is, teachers ought to be trained to reflect on what kind of teachers they are, (their values and beliefs) and how they became that way.

SUMMARY/CONCLUSIONS

This chapter has focused on the role that the school plays in the process of socialization. We have discussed the way socialization takes place within the family from various perspectives —the functionalist perspective, and various other social psychological theories, such as the psychoanalytic, cognitive, and social learning theories. The theoretical perspectives we have drawn from to explain the informal process of socialization are that of symbolic interaction, phenomenology, and interpretive sociology.

Following the discussion on the process of socialization, we have explained how teachers' expectations affect students' school performance. We have discussed how teachers use unquestioned, commonsense knowledge about effective teaching to interpret and respond to their pupils' behaviours, and how teacher typifications of pupils' behaviours play an important role in categorizing pupils for the purpose of classroom organization.

The school as an agent of moral and political socialization was also discussed. Here we saw how national identity and social control are part of the informal process of socialization. Again, the emphasis was on the importance of how educators question this process. The discussion on the hidden curriculum, peer groups, and popular culture pointed to the significance of these factors on students' social experiences and learning achievements in educational settings. Finally, we presented various strategies for generating discussions on educational and social change.

As we have seen from the description of the Alternate School in Chapter 4, what educators decide about education is important, but what students decide is even more important. A discussion of the problems facing young people today can be incorporated into classroom practice, curriculum design, the structure of the educational system, and teacher training programs. The final chapter provides an overview of reform movements in education and proposes some ways to move forward.

KEY TERMS

cognitive perspective	mentoring	socialization; primary and secondary
generalized other	moral socialization	
id, ego, and superego	pluralism	taken-for-granted perspective
internalization	political socialization	tracking
intersubjectivity	significant other	typifications
melting pot	social learning theory	

DISCUSSION QUESTIONS

1. Providing examples, discuss how the hidden curriculum has affected your schooling experience.
2. Discuss how peer groups and popular culture have affected your social and academic experiences in school.
3. Explain the role of teachers' expectations and discuss how these have affected your own social and academic experiences.
4. What do you think should be included in the curriculum of teacher training programs that could lead to equality in education?

RECOMMENDED READINGS/REFERENCES

Apple, M. W. (1979). *Ideology and curriculum*. Boston: Routledge Kegan Paul.

Apple, M. W., & Christian-Smith, L. K. (Eds.) (1991). *The politics of the textbook*. New York: Routledge.

Aronowitz, S., & Giroux, H. (1985). *Education under siege*. New York: Bergin & Garvey.

Aronowitz, S., & Giroux, H. (1993). *Education still under siege*. New York: Bergin & Garvey.

Ballantine, J. (1983). *The sociology of education: A systematic analysis*. New Jersey: Prentice Hall.

Beyer, L. (1987). What knowledge is of most worth in teacher education? In J. Smyth (Ed.), *Educating teachers: changing the nature of pedagogical knowledge* (pp. 19-14). New York: Falmer Press.

Clarke, B., & Trow, M. (1966). The organization context. In T. Newcomb, & E. Wilson (Eds.), *College peer groups: Problems and prospects for research* (pp.17–70). Chicago: Aldine,.

Coleman, J. (1961). *The adolescent society.* New York: Free Press.

Cooley, C. H. (1956). *Human nature and the social order.* Glencoe, IL: Free Press.

Dreeben, R. (1968). *On what is learned in school.* Reading, Mass.: Addison-Wesley.

Durkheim, E. (1961). *Moral education.* New York: The Free Press.

Giroux, H., & Simon, R. (1989). Popular culture and critical pedagogy. In H. Giroux, & P. McLaren (Eds.), *Critical pedagogy, the state and cultural struggle* (pp. 236–251). New York: State University of New York Press.

Gore, J. (1993). *The struggle for pedagogies.* New York: Routledge.

Hargreaves, D. H., Hester, S. K., & Mellor, F. J. (1975). *Deviance in classrooms.* London: Routledge and Keegan Paul.

Jackson, P. (1968). *Life in classrooms.* New York: Holt, Rinehart & Wilson.

Liston, D., & Zeichner, K. (1987). Critical pedagogy and teacher education. *Journal of education, 169* (3), 117–137.

Liston, D., & K. Zeichner. (1991). *Teacher education and the social conditions of schooling.* New York: Routledge.

Mackie, M. (1994). Socialization. In R. Hagedorn (Ed.) *Sociology* (5th ed.) (pp. 89-120). Toronto: Harcourt Brace and Company.

Mead, G. (1934). *Mind, self and society.* Chicago: University or Chicago Press.

Mifflen, F. J., & Mifflen, S. C. (1982). *The sociology of education: Canada and beyond.* Calgary: Detselig.

Nathanson, M. (1970). Phenomenology and typification: A study in the philosophy of Alfred Schutz. *Social Research, 37,* 3–4 & 6–8.

Parsons, T. (1967) The school class as a social system. In P. Roge (Ed.). *The study of society* (pp. 647–665). New York: Random House.

Schutz, A. (1973). *Collected Papers: The problem of social reality, vol 1.* The Hague: Martinus Nijhoff.

Sheehan, N., & Fullan, M. (1995). Teacher education in Canada: A case study of British Columbia and Ontario. In M. Wideen, & P. Grimmett (Eds.), *Changing times in teacher education* (pp.89–101). Bristol: Falmer Press.

Smyth, J. (1989). A critical pedagogy of classroom practice. *Journal of curriculum studies, 21 (*6), 483–502.

Tom, A. (1987). Replacing pedagogical knowledge with pedagogical questions. In J. Smyth (Ed.), *Educating teachers: Changing the nature of pedagogical knowledge* (pp. 9–17). Philadelphia: Falmer Press.

Tom, A. (1995). Stirring the embers: Reconsidering the structure of teacher education programs. In M. Wideen, & P. Grimmet (Eds.), *Changing times in teacher education* (pp. 117–131). Bristol: Falmer Press.

Wagner, H. (Ed.). (1970). *Alfred Schutz on phenomenology and social relations.* Chicago: University of Chicago Press.

6

EDUCATION AND CHANGE

Chapter Objectives

Education and change is a large topic that could be the central theme of an entire book. In this chapter, we emphasize some of the key issues and problems in education in Canada today, examining these in a context of change. To do so, we look at some of the steps that the Canadian federal and provincial governments have taken to provide a climate for each province's educational system in response to increasingly diverse school populations. Next, we describe Canada's contribution to reform in the field of second-language teaching. We then examine reform movements, past and present, to learn what they have intended or do intend to achieve. Finally, looking into the future, we raise some questions for students and educators to consider as they enter the twenty-first century.

We do not presume to suggest which social policies should be developed for educational change, but we do hope to alert our readers to the importance of questioning proposals for change and, once they become practising educators, to insist on being fully consulted at every step of the change process.

REFORM AND POLICY MAKING IN CANADIAN EDUCATION

Policies are written statements that are intended as guidelines for making decisions and acting under specific circumstances. In education, policies may apply to an entire system or they may be specific to a particular school board or school. Although policies are not laws, they sometimes are transformed into laws or even charters, such as the Canadian Charter of Rights and Freedoms (1982), which enshrine peoples' rights. A language policy may not be sufficient to guarantee access to French-language schooling in all parts of Canada, but the language laws of Quebec (Bill 101, for example) ensure access to English-language schools for children whose parents were educated in English in Canada. The same law, however, restricts access to English schools to all others. Policies, therefore, decide who can go to school and where, what is to be taught, who may teach, and how students are to be treated. Unlike laws, which can be enforced, policies cannot be enforced except through persuasion or the establishment of consensus.

Policy making always takes place in a context of competing interests. For instance, in education in Canada, there is a constant tension between the need for practices that apply equally to all, and the need to respond to exceptional individual circumstances. And although North American culture is primarily individualistic, not communal, in its orientation, there is much concern with the topic of equality. In Western culture, educators tend to see such matters as child development, achievement in school, and the development of personal identity as essentially a phenomenon of the individual (Hatch, 1995). In many other parts of the world, the primary focus is on the group or community that the child belongs to, and individual wants and concerns are secondary to the needs of the group (Serpell, 1993). This difference between an individualistic orientation and a communal orientation was illustrated simply by the title of an African visiting scholar's presentation at a university in Montreal, *I am Because We Are* (Mpofu, 1996).

Article 33 of the Quebec Civil Code provides legal exceptions to the language law, which otherwise applies to all. In addition to the provisions in the law that allows for children who have severe learning problems to be transferred to English schools, should the school so advise or a parent request, Article 33 states,

> Every decision concerning a child shall be taken in light of the child's interests and the respect of his rights. Consideration is given, in addition to the moral, intellectual, emotional and material needs of the child, to the child's age, health, personality and family environment, and to the other aspects of his situation.

Policies are made through a political process of negotiating competing interests, thus the influence of politics in education is inevitable. The political process is one in which those with the most power influence those with less power. Thus, as suggested above, many changes in education are made in a context of competing values, with one group lobbying for their set of values, and another group lobbying for a different set of values. While this process is democratic, there are indications that policies in education are increasingly influenced by powerful corporate interests. At some point, the key stakeholders in education—teachers, school administrators, parents, and students—appear to have been excluded from the decision-making process. Thus one of the central problems in education today is to ensure that the voices of those most closely *affected* by the decisions that are being made have a chance to be heard and to influence the process, too.

Who should participate in the policy-making process? Should control over policy be localized at a community level, or centralized at a higher level? These are the key questions regarding education policy. Clearly, there are some decisions that require the expertise of highly educated experts, while other issues are more appropriately decided at the level of the community, or by parents. But there are many grey areas, too. For example, during a time of cutbacks in funding to schools, who should decide what is to be cut from the curriculum? How widespread is the position that mathematics and language arts are more important than music and art?

Although the trend in Canada and elsewhere towards increased *local control* of schools might appear to be a healthy resistance to the concurrent and opposing trend of distant, corporate control, it may not be so. Should parents and students decide the content of the curriculum, for example? Should parents have the right to decide that the local public school teach half the day in a language other than English or French? What are the limits? What kind of society do we envision? How do we deal with diversity?

In a diverse, multicultural society such as Canada there are bound to be disagreements and conflicts over what is best for children and young people. One of the ways this inherent conflict is dealt with is to allow a range of different types of schools in any single community. In Toronto and Montreal, for example, one finds many private schools, most of which cater to high-income families, many of which are modelled after the elite "public" (private) schools of Britain, most notably in their requirement of school uniforms. There are also numerous semiprivate religious schools designed to provide education in an environment where parents' religious convictions are not only supported but taught as well. The fact that most private schools receive government funding, provided they follow government regulations in matters of curriculum, examinations, and access (i.e. comply with the terms of Bill 101 in Quebec), is an indication of the extent to which there is consensus in Canadian society that such schools should exist (McAndrew, 1995).

The foregoing reminds us that although education is entirely a matter of the provinces the Canadian government has, from time to time, played a leading role in defining what the overriding norms and attitudes ought to be in a multicultural society. Here we have in mind Canada's **policy of multiculturalism**, put forth in 1971 by former Prime Minister Pierre Trudeau.

Canada's Policy of Multiculturalism

The overall intention of this policy was to promote **unity in diversity**. The policy was a response to the upheaval that Canadian society had experienced in the 1960s with the Quiet Revolution in Quebec, and it was a reaction to the civil rights movement in the United States as well. Both movements were about the rights of minorities, which hitherto had been left out of the mainstream of society. Unfortunately, for French-speaking people living in Quebec, the policy did not respond to their needs for recognition, which were not considered to be equivalent to the needs of Canada's ethnic minorities. It is important to remember here that Canada officially recognizes two founding groups—the French and the English. The French-speaking population has been a numerical minority in the country as a whole and a numerical majority within the province of Quebec, but the two linguistic groups are officially equal in status. Thus, the Quiet Revolution was about francophones taking charge in the province of Quebec, about redistributing power from the predominantly an-glophone corporate elite, as well as from the Roman Catholic Church through widespread secularization of many institutions particularly the education system. Prior to 1964, when the first Ministère de l'education du Québec was established, the church had held full control over education, except for the small Protestant minority. For the French, the Quiet Revolution was, therefore, about becoming masters in their own house (maîtres chez nous), not about being one of many ethnic or linguistic minorities in the overall context of Canada. The separatist movement in Québec, headed by René Lévesque, Lucien Bouchard, and others, was (and still is) concerned with creating *un nation,* which in French refers to a collective sense of iden-tity based on common roots and an attachment to the land.

Perhaps because of the complexity of the Canadian situation, the policy of multicultur-alism should be seen as an attempt that has met with both success and failure. The policy was intended to provide a climate in which the Canadian mosaic, as first described in 1965 by John Porter, could be nurtured. To emphasize further, this policy was intended to direct the pop-ulace towards tolerance of differences and to increase equality. That is, the intention was to confirm an ideology of cultural pluralism as a suitable way for Canadian society to pro-ceed and as an alternative to the tendency towards assimilation that had marked the earlier part of the century in Canada and which remains the prevailing ideology in the United States. Although formal education, as stated earlier, is under provincial jurisdiction, the policy provides a *definition of the situation* for provincial ministries and local school boards to emulate in their own policies. MacAndrew quotes former Prime Minister Trudeau as fol-lows,

> ...there cannot be one cultural policy for Canadians of British and French origin, another for the original peoples, and yet a third for all the others. For although there are two official lan-guages there is no official culture, nor does any ethnic group take precedence over any other ....A policy of multiculturalism within a bilingual framework commits itself to the government as the most suitable means of assuring the cultural freedom of Canadians...the government will assist members of all cultural groups to overcome cultural barriers to full participation in Canadian society (McAndrew, 1987 p. 145.).

Although each province has interpreted the policy according to its own priorities and tra-ditions, diversity continues to present a set of complex issues to Canada's education systems. As we saw in Chapter 3, the debates over what constitutes an appropriate curriculum and how far schools should go in adapting to cultural differences have yet to be resolved.

LANGUAGE OF EDUCATION REFORM IN CANADA

Related to the foregoing was the early French immersion movement that began in 1964 in Quebec and later spread to other parts of Canada (Lambert & Tucker, 1972). The move-ment started as an experiment of a group of English-speaking parents from the Montreal suburb of St. Lambert who were determined that, in a officially bilingual country, their children would become bilingual. Most of the parents had been educated in the English-Protestant system, where French had been taught for one hour each day, usually by non-francophones. They had not mastered the language well enough either to form friendships or to use it in the workplace. At work, it was the French-speaking people who switched to English, not vice versa.

After consulting with experts in neurology and psychology to reassure themselves that their children would not be damaged by the "experiment," the parents started a school where the language of instruction from kindergarten to grade three was French. This was called **total, early immersion**. The long-term, stated objective was to improve relations between French and English speakers by improving the ability of children from English-speaking homes to live and work using the French language. The aim was to accomplish this without loss of English language skills. That is, the early French-immersion programs were not intended to be **transitional bilingual programs** that would shift the children to the exclusive use of French, but rather were intended to guarantee **first language maintenance**.

From the start, this experimental program was carefully evaluated by researchers from McGill University. Within a few years, the program slowly expanded and eventually found a home in a regular school. By the early 1970s, early French-immersion programs had been started in other schools in Montreal, however, they remained designated "experimental" for 16 years, in part because no one was willing to accept the consequences of potentially negative long-term effects. Thus it took at least this long for the first cohorts of children from this program to graduate from high school, enter university, and obtain jobs (where the use of French was necessary). Eventually, the positive results of program evaluations and good publicity fostered similar programs across Canada, where they persist to this day (*The Gazette*, March 20, 1999; Lambert & Tucker, 1972; Genesee,1987). Today an estimated three hundred thousand children are enrolled in French-immersion programs at any one time.

Many would argue that French immersion programs have not altered the character of French-English relations in Canadian society at large. However, it is important to remember that there have been concurrent waves of separatist-motivated political unrest in Quebec over the past 30 years. Thus we cannot say whether the experiment was successful or not, either at a national or a provincial level. We can say, though, that approximately two million Canadians attended French-immersion programs over the last thirty years and are now able to work and live in both official languages.

French-immersion programs are not the only language programs that protect and promote diversity in Canada. In Ontario, heritage-language programs are housed in schools and offered in an extended-day format. Although these programs have been cut back due to budget reductions, at one time children had access to instruction in 26 different mother-tongue languages (Ghosh & Ray, 1995). In Quebec, government-sponsored programs offer first-language literacy and other training to those who speak neither French nor English, as well as after-school language programs for children who speak neither French nor English at home. And in addition to language programs, there are many other federally sponsored and provincially based efforts that celebrate diversity, such as Black history month, Caribbean festivals, and First Nations days. However, a study of multiculturalism at the level of the school in one Montreal school board found teachers, school administrators, and school board officers reluctant to establish local official policies on multiculturalism because they believed that they were already doing what was expected of them (Cleghorn & Lowerison, 1991).

REFORM MOVEMENTS IN EDUCATION

The history of education in the Western world has been marked by a series of reform movements, each of which have had dual objectives. On the one hand, the aim has been to expand and improve the delivery of educational services. On the other hand, there has been an attempt through change in education to address society's social and economic problems, and in this way to improve society as a whole. That is, change in education has always coincided with a perceived need for **social change**. What has never been clear is the *direction* of change. Does change in society indicate a need for change in schooling practices, or do problems within education itself point to the need for changes within the larger society? The 1999 shootings at schools in Colorado and Alberta provide examples of how inextricably linked educational and societal problems are. Some people see violence in schools as stemming from children's exposure to violence on television; some see the problem as a result of a breakdown in school discipline, capable of being solved by making school uniforms compulsory, for example. Still others see the problem as fundamentally linked through warfare to the expression of international power relations, which obscure the actions of those in top positions of power and are rarely openly questioned.

When considering change, it is important to ask *who* decides *what* is to change, *how* the decisions will be made, and *who* is to benefit by the change. That is, to what extent are reforms in education *politically charged* decisions, whether they be large, involving the whole education system, or small, involving the curriculum, for example? In the sections that follow, we examine both large- and small-scale reform efforts.

Early Reform Movements

One of the first reform movements coupled the rise of compulsory schooling in the nineteenth century with society's need for a compliant, reliable work force to support manufacturing. Bowles and Gintis (1976) demonstrated convincingly that compulsory schooling was not only intended to rescue the poor from their plight but, more accurately, to guarantee the continued prosperity of factory owners (who frequently were members of local school boards). The concern was less with educating than with the development of specific morals (norms of the workplace), such as valuing punctuality and respecting authority.

With the increasing number of white-collar jobs and the development of large-scale capitalist production in the early twentieth century, secondary schooling also began to expand. The elites who were in charge of the system needed to find ways to get people to *want* to do what *had* to be done, and to counter the threat of social unrest, perceived at that time to come mainly from the working-class and immigrant groups. Progressive changes in the previously all-classical curriculum were made available to children of the middle class, and in due course vocational education in comprehensive high schools, with their many different academic tracks, provided an "acceptable" channel for working-class youth. That is, as the **division of labour** became increasingly complex, so too was it necessary to stratify the school system. As discussed in earlier chapters, this and other forms of tracking were supported and legitimized through the use of supposedly objective testing procedures.

With the development of mass and universal schooling came demands for equality of opportunity. According to the functionalist view of Collins (1979) and others, **status competition** between groups fuelled educational expansion through demands for formal training and qualifications. In due course, as the general levels of education increased so too did the development of programs at the university and graduate levels, hence the spiralling of **qualificationism** that Dore (1976) referred to in his book *The Diploma Disease*. As the average levels of education rise more and more credentials are needed to qualify for even the most unskilled jobs. This is equally the case in the industrialized countries as it is in the less-developed countries that Dore speaks of.

Deschooling in the 1960s and 1970s

A few educators began to question the obvious shortcomings of mass schooling, particularly, but not only, as these relate to the educational outcomes for children from working-class homes as well as from immigrant and racial minority backgrounds. John Holt's *Why Children Fail,* A. S. Neill's *Summerhill,* and Ivan Illich's *Deschooling Society* became compulsory reading in education faculties and teacher training programs as well as popular among the public during the 1960s. They suggested alternative ways of schooling that were then put into practice, supported often by parents who wanted a more egalitarian and humanistic schooling for their children. Their vision was of a fully democratic society, free of conflict, organized through goodwill.

Free schools were established outside the regular school system (usually by parent groups) and organized along democratic lines. Decisions about curriculum, behaviour, dress code, grading, and discipline were decided collectively by students, teachers, parents, and school administrators. Teachers were to guide rather than dictate children's learning. Children were encouraged to explore, work and study, motivated intrinsically and with a measure of control over what and how they learned.

There are several reasons why the majority of free schools did not survive very long. Like most reform movements, the free schools had built-in contradictions. For example, despite their non-elitist aims, they were essentially private schools, dependent upon tuition, which most parents from the working class could ill afford. Thus the majority of children who attended free schools came from well-educated, middle-class families, that is, from families that already enjoyed the social status that could be passed on to their children through ascription. Another reason for the demise of most free schools was that students, teachers, parents and administrators had to spend inordinate amounts of time in meetings, trying to come to a consensus about how to run the school. Not only did this often lead to bitter infighting and disagreements, but it took more time than many were willing to commit. Eventually, the organization of free schools became as hierarchical as that of regular schools, with a few people holding positions of power.

In contrast to the free school movement, **open schools** were and are part of the regular system. They are distinguished by small-group instruction, sometimes in classrooms without walls, sometimes with mixed-age groupings. The pace of instruction and learning is determined by student interest and inclination, rather than the sounding of a bell every thirty-five minutes.

Interaction between teachers and students and among the students is relatively free, with behaviour controlled, as much as possible, through cooperation and persuasion. Instruction is based on the constructivist philosophy discussed previously in Chapter 3.

Unfortunately, advocates of open schools and open classrooms underestimated the effects of noise on the ability to teach and learn and overestimated the likelihood that children and adolescents would control their own behaviour. In fact, for many children in open classrooms the definition of the situation was ambiguous, since the rules were not clearly stated. More important, perhaps, is the fact that when the rules governing interaction and other aspects of behaviour are implicit, a shared understanding of those rules requires that the participants share a common culture. When classes are homogeneous the students may more easily understand the often unstated rules; however, when students come from diverse ethnic, relgious, and language backgrounds they may bring different expectations to school and, interpreting school events on the basis of their expectations, they behave accordingly. There may be many apparent "infractions" of the rules, stemming from cross-cultural misunderstandings, making it seem necessary for the rules to be spelled out and enforced. In this case, the egalitarian ideals of the open school and open classroom may be quickly abandoned.

There are other parallels between schooling and the requirements of the workplace that prevail even today to some extent. In schools that are organized in traditional ways (and these are the majority), students do not get to choose what or when they learn, nor are they permitted to decide the pace of their work. At the ring of a bell students are expected to turn interest on and off, to make rapid shifts from one subject to another. They are taught in a group, yet they are not permitted to interact with their peers unless directed to do so by the teacher, even though teachers are educated to value the individual and to create child-centred classrooms. According to Hurn (1993) these very characteristics, when found in the workplace, are associated with job dissatisfaction and low morale. How, then, can we expect schools that are thus organized to be successful in their mission? Despite the above-described efforts to reform the nature of schooling, little actual change has taken place.

Curricular Reform

The first step in any reform in education ought to entail a careful study of the success or failure of similar reforms carried out elsewhere. Unfortunately, such study rarely takes place, since reforms have less to do with education than with politics. That is, reforms in education tend to be implemented for political reasons. In the case described below, there had been pressure from the political right to raise academic standards; however, there was no solid evidence to suggest that standards had fallen. In fact, concerns about falling standards sometimes mask an uneasiness with an increasingly diverse student population (Freebody & Welch, 1993).

The case of New Zealand's attempt to reform its science curriculum provides some important lessons for Canada. The goal was to raise standards by introducing greater accountability into the system by using clearly defined set standards. This was to be accomplished with a new science curriculum developed on the principles of a constructivist philosophy (Sanders, 1999).

Some Lessons for Canada from New Zealand

New Zealand's effort to implement a new science curriculum is a case in point. The proposal met with much approval from teachers because of its constructivist philosophy, and the teaching approaches it advocated. The document applied research and theory about effective teaching and learning as well as a coherent framework for science content from the primary level to the end of the secondary level. The curriculum was to focus on situations that would be familiar to the learners allowing them to build on what they already knew. Financial support was to provide teacher aides to schools with English-as-a-second-language learners. The plan appeared to be ideal. Nevertheless, problems arose, primarily on implementation.

While primary-school teachers were comfortable with the constructivist, holistic, and integrated approach to teaching science, which even incorporated drama and poetry, the secondary-school teachers felt that this approach was inappropriate for teaching "real" science. Also, teachers who were not already using a constructivist philosophy in their teaching felt insecure and were not able to make the switch easily. Other teachers felt that the science content was "watered down." Teachers were mainly concerned with the contrast between what appeared to be a loosely defined but skills-oriented emphasis in the content and strictly defined achievement objectives (set standards) and assessment procedures.

Because children decided what topics to explore on the basis of interest, it was nearly impossible to ensure that all of the required content was covered within each of the stated objectives.

In order to document that the objectives were being achieved, teachers were continuously engaged in assessment. This increased their workload, taking up valuable teaching time. In effect, the system of continuous assessment, which was tied to the set standards, did not fit with the constructivist philosophy of the proposed program.

Another problem with set standards and their assessment was that they discriminated against both low-achieving and high-achieving students. Low achievers were denied the range of standards suitable to their needs, while high achievers were not stretched beyond the upper standard. Once they had achieved at the required pass level there was no need to aim higher.

Instead of garnering the support of teachers, the pressures that the new curriculum imposed alienated them from the change process. The new program was implemented too quickly and without adequate financial support for professional development, for materials, or for the added administration involved in assessment. Disenchantment among the teachers spread and led to strikes. The plan was eventually dropped.

Source: Adapted from Sanders, M. (1999). Reprinted with permission.

NONTRADITIONAL SCHOOLING AT THE START OF 2000

Several concurrent trends throughout the world are resulting in a rethinking of the traditional forms of schooling, their purposes, and limitations. First, there is a trend everywhere towards local control or decentralization. Second, there are increasing concerns about the ineffectiveness of the traditional model of schooling for large numbers of young people as evidenced by high drop out rates in Canadian secondary schools. In many parts of the still-developing world, the irrelevance of a western model of schooling to local circumstances results in early drop out and the persistence of extremely low levels of literacy. Simultaneously, we see an increase in concern over **internal and external efficiency**, cost benefits, and school quality (quality of "inputs," quality of results, as well as quality of the instructional process) (Heneveld, 1994). We ask, however, whether the transfer of responsibility for management, control, and content of schooling to the local level will result in greater equality. What measures will insure that sometimes desperate local socioeconomic conditions do not simply become reflected in local schools? How can we promote more community involvement in the schools without bringing about complete chaos? Clearly, there is a need to take into consideration a diversity of community purposes in schooling while ensuring that everyone has an equal chance to reenter the system at the levels of higher education, where centralized control tends to resume, due mainly to the need for national economic planning as well as the need for an educated populace that can assume national, corporate, and other positions of leadership and responsibility.

Deschooling Revisited

Recently a few educators have put forth a renewed vision of schooling that takes place outside the school and classroom (Hern 1996; Meighan, 1997). We might call this **deschooling** revisited; however, it appears that what is being proposed is not so much in response to dissatisfaction with the way schools are as much as an acknowledgment of a possible impending reality. Norman Henchey, for example, recently stated in the press that if technology is going to be the main transmitter of knowledge then there is no reason for children to be in school. Theoretically, they can be at home (in front of a computer), at the local library (in front of a computer) or anywhere else (at a friend's home, or in another city visiting an absent parent, in front of a computer). While such a vision might be fully supported by parents who are in favour of home schooling and are willing to act as teachers or supervisors, it is short on the recognition of all those other things that are taught and learned in school (for better or for worse) through the hidden curriculum, through interaction with peers, and through the process of becoming familiar with one of society's main bureaucratic institutions. It does not take long to come to the conclusion that such a plan is unworkable on a large scale, especially in today's world where most parents work. As noted in Chapter 1, the school has an important custodial function to play for society at large.

Home Schooling

What is **home schooling**, who does it, and why? Is it effective? A 1993 report on home schooling in Canada showed that about ten thousand children were registered as being home schooled, while estimates are as high as thirty thousand being unofficially home schooled (Smith, 1993).

Parents who choose to home school their children are a diverse lot, however, it is evident that most are fairly well educated, if not very well educated. Several reasons are cited for home schooling. First is general dissatisfaction with schools. Schools are perceived as places where creativity and curiosity are squashed rather than nurtured. Schools are seen as impersonal places where communication tends to be one way: from teacher to students. Schools are seen to be places where groupings by grade and age are unnatural. The belief is that home schooling counters all of these features while promoting self-discipline, self-directed learning, and the personal confidence and self-esteem that comes with a young person's mastery of ideas and situations.

Home schooling is not for everyone. Although it is an ideal way for parents who are living in isolated communities or in foreign countries to ensure that their children keep up with their regularly schooled peers, through correspondence, for example, home schooling is best served by a community that is rich in resources such as libraries, museums, and local businesses that are willing to participate. Since most parents are not sufficiently knowledgeable about every subject to feel confident teaching it, they need to organize themselves to fill the gaps. Home schooling can be hard work, requiring full-time dedication on the part of a parent. On the other hand, neither the parent nor the child is bound to the schedule of a school day, so schooling at home can be flexible.

Questions typically arise among the home schooling sceptics about two matters: the development of home-schooled children's social skills, and whether or not they can compete with regularly schooled students on standardized tests of achievement. To this the advocates of home schooling simply ask if most parents would not prefer to avoid what they refer to as the *tyranny of the peer group*. Although home-schooled children tend to be independent thinkers, there is no evidence to suggest that they become social isolates. And finally, home schooling is just as or more effective than traditional schooling as measured by standardized achievement tests such as the Scholastic Achievement Test (SAT) (Hern 1996; Meighan, 1997).

The Environment as Curriculum Content

There remains the possibility of modifying the ways that traditional schools operate, incorporating some of the many positive features of home schooling. Here we have in mind a systematic attempt to link what goes on in school with the content and events of the real world outside of school. In this vision there is a close collaboration between schools and other institutions and businesses in society. This is a vision where **hands-on learning** takes on a more literal meaning. In this model, children would have a well-planned program of instruction coupled with practical experience that over time would familiarize them with many kinds of jobs and professions while, ideally, providing meaning to what is learned in school. They would, for example, become the plumber's helper, the scientist's observer, the courtroom reporter, the volunteer in the old people's home. Their mathematics skills would find application in a bank or grocery store, their science lessons would find meaning in a pharmaceutical lab, their knowledge of plants and animals would literally come to life at a garden centre or veterinary clinic, for example.

Critics might point out that this vision would entail a complete restructuring of the way schools are presently organized as well as a much more complete involvement of the community, including parents, than presently exists.

THE REIGN OF TECHNOLOGY

Many readers are likely to think of technology when the future is mentioned. As much as new technology might appear to offer solutions to many of the problems in society and our system of education, we suggest that never before has there been a time when a more human, nontechnological approach to educational change is *also* needed. Never before has it been so necessary to incorporate a critical and reflective stance into everything we do— in the policies we develop, in the way we educate our teachers, and in the way we interact with students. As the world becomes a global village, environmentally, technologically and culturally, there is a risk that no one will be in charge, that decisions will be driven by capitalistic considerations, and that the multinational corporate world will, in effect, make decisions for us. In our view, this is the antithesis of democracy. Recent public controversy over media corporations donating computer equipment to schools in exchange for a few minutes of televised current events (accompanied by advertisements) suggests that we may already have reached this stage. We hope that this section will cause the reader to think about some possible alternatives to this bleak scenario.

At the start of the twenty-first century the kind of change that most educators are grappling with has to do with advances in technology and its influence on the educational process at all levels of the system. According to Henchey (1987, p. 37),

> Modern technology is changing how and where we work, what work we do, how we communicate with others, how we play, and, at a deeper level, how we think, how we see ourselves, and what we value. It is also changing how, where, and when we learn, as well as why and what we need to learn.

While this situation applies in every industrialized country, it is at the forefront of recommendations for reforms in Canadian classrooms. A recent newspaper report entitled "Laptops or Textbooks?" illustrates the need to proceed cautiously. The article describes a proposal to introduce the use of computers for 25 percent of class time in the grade four classrooms of one school board in Montreal. The sixty thousand dollar initiative, backed by one of the major computer software corporations, is described as an exciting project by a senior officer of the school board, while the president of the local union thinks the money would be better spent on badly needed textbooks (The Gazette, May 12, 1999). This account demonstrates the kind of controversy that surrounds certain changes in education as well as the fact that decisions tend to be made without proper **needs assessment**, public debate, or consultation with the "stakeholders" and without a full discussion of the potential consequences for society at large. Furthermore, as previously stated, those who will be required to implement the change—the teachers—are rarely involved in any significant way in making these kinds of decisions. We might then ask, Who will be blamed if the outcomes are minimal and do not match the investment? As suggested in Chapter 1, probably the teacher.

Further to the foregoing, our position is that extensive corporate involvement in education is likely to increase inequality. In the proposal for the extensive use of computers in elementary classrooms in Montreal, parents were "willing" to pay a $15 per month rental fee.. But what about the parents who cannot afford this? The article also reports that 250 schools worldwide have implemented such a computer program. Similarly, we ask, in which part of the world are these schools located. It is important for educators to realize that inequality is a global as well as a local problem, one that involves us all.

The new linkages between corporations and the universities pose an additional concern. We ask how these changes are being implemented and what effect they have on the traditional value of academic work. To what extent is academic freedom relinquished when research is funded by the private sector? To what extent does the knowledge created within universities remain a universally available resource, or does it become available only to those with high-tech access, thereby, in some minds, becoming indistinguishable from *information*? (Buchbinder & Newson, 1994).

Technology has thus become an issue in education. Understanding this issue requires that educators be **technologically literate,** and this goes far beyond the implementation and use of computers in classrooms. Referring to technological artefacts Fleming states

> ...studying technological artefacts is studying the mind and culture of the mind that produced the artefact. The artefact is a text, allowing for a critical "reading" of the culture that produced it (1990, p. 54).

Fleming goes on to point out that it is important for educators to understand the many dimensions of technology. For example, most of us think of the hardware when we think of computers in classrooms. Some might also consider the process of manufacturing the hardware, or the income associated with the development of software. But hardware and software are developed within a **sociotechnical system,** which includes people, machines, and other resources. Finally, there is a sociotechnical system *of use*. To be fully literate, then, in a technological society, a person needs to be aware of the nature of technological knowledge, the nature of the decisions that are being considered, and the range of possible consequences:

> A technologically literate person must...understand the relationship between technology and social change...must "read" the artefact to find within it the set of societal assumptions that may cause the artefact to effect change in the society. To do this, one must conceptualize technology as a social organization. (Wynne, 1988, pp. 147–167).

Fleming notes that social change is driven by those who have access to the economic and political resources to implement a new technology. When a new technology causes social strain, for example, by depleting resources for something else that is also valued, then the issue becomes politically and socially charged with a counterelite's experts demanding evaluations and legislation to control the new technology.

The foregoing suggests that there are unpredictable implications for the organization of schooling as well as for what is learned in school and how teaching will continue to be carried out. Some have suggested that an "information overload" will force schools and other formal organizations to restructure along decentralized, "flat" lines. That is, it is proposed that the hierarchical organization of schooling will be replaced by horizontal networks of people who share the same viewpoints and manage to get along on the basis of informal rules (norms)(Fukuyama, 1999). Although there are bound to be changes, especially in the technical means of delivering knowledge, we remind our readers that schooling is essentially a conservative institution in society, an institution marked more by what are sometimes called "cultural lags" than by innovations. Thus, it remains to be seen how deep into the structures of schooling the now hotly debated changes will go.

NEW DIRECTIONS

Since the 1980s, most schools in urban parts of Canada, the United States, Great Britain, and other industrialized countries have become obviously diverse—culturally, racially, linguistically, and religiously. At the same time, the authority of the school seems to have declined, drop out rates have increased, and the potential for violence appears to be everywhere. While there are some who would use these situations as evidence that academic standards have dropped (Freebody & Welch, 1993), we disagree. That there are problems everywhere is evident; however, we believe that the causes of the problems are extremely complex, tied most often to local expressions of global problems, with their solutions more appropriately worked out at the local level, in collaboration with the stakeholders—educators, community leaders, parents, and students. The following accounts provide some promising examples of what may be possible.

The Inclusive Curriculum

Talking about change and bringing change about are two very different things. Although there are many advocates of change in education, history shows that very little change takes place from one decade to the next. In reality, there is much resistance to change, mainly because once privileges have been gained few are willing to give them away. If power were truly shared it would not be power. The central problem, then, is in persuading people that with change everyone stands to gain, no one need lose. What might be lost, and the source of much resistance to change is illegitimate power: power that depends on the oppression of others in order to be sustained. To clarify what we mean, we must turn once again to Freire.

When people learn to think critically and to speak up when they believe that something is unfair they are doing what needs to be done to transform their world (Freire, 1968). What Freire calls the practice of freedom is basic to the **inclusive curriculum**, sometimes called the **antibias curriculum**. In this model, the goals are to ensure full access to education for everyone, for everyone to have the right and assistance to develop self-confidence, for everyone to have the courage and ability to stand up against injustice. The inclusive curriculum finds a balance between respecting difference and rejecting behaviour that excludes and thwarts opportunities for full development. It seeks to provide a context for every child and student to realize their own potential while not devaluing the results of those who have less potential than others.

The inclusive curriculum aims to find a balance between respecting difference, creating environments that include all levels of ability and maintaining high expectations for achieving individual potentials. The inclusive curriculum is for all: children of colour, those whose first language is neither English nor French, boys and girls, and those with differences in physical and intellectual ability. It assumes that all children's development is harmed when negative bias towards "other" is experienced, whether they themselves feel inferior or superior in the equation.

Throughout the world there is a growing awareness that standardized, ability-grouped schooling successfully serves fewer and fewer children as classrooms become increasingly multiethnic, as poverty encroaches upon communities everywhere and, indeed, as expectations change. The inclusive curriculum aims to create learning situations that are both informed by and reflective of this growing diversity of needs. The curriculum content seeks to avoid tokenism (such as celebrating certain festivals without reference to the lifestyles and daily traditions of the chosen group, or telling a story now and then about a child in a wheelchair), and instead reflects both the diversity of experiences of the children in the classroom and the diversity of children in other parts of the world. In practice this implies a number of changes from the traditional, isolated unit of the classroom.

First, it seeks to involve the families of the children and the participation of the local community. Teachers in regular classrooms have not traditionally been trained to work as collaborators. Nevertheless, parents are invaluable as a prime source of accurate information about their children, their traditions, life styles, history, and belief systems. They can shed useful light on new ways of teaching even the most mundane subject, reflecting their children's culture and experience as well as their own. In this way their involvement in the educational, social, and cultural activities in the school can be seen as a welcome addition to existing resources, rather than an intrusion to or disruption of the learning environment. The larger community, too, is involved. Whether the school receives regular visits from community members or the children are regularly involved in projects with sections of the community, the effects are positive; community involvement enlarges horizons and builds links that endure. Inclusive curriculum implies children and adults working and learning together.

Much can be learned from recent developments in inclusive curriculum for the early years. *The Anti-Bias Curriculum*, first published in 1989, was the first how-to book on inclusive practice and is still a very comprehensive and adaptable resource. There are also any number of initiatives that have been undertaken to humanize and contextualize children's early learning experiences in this way. Some of the most enduring and innovative are in the High/Scope preschool curriculum in the USA, the Te Whariki project in New Zealand, and the Reggio Emilia schools in Italy.

Second, the inclusive curriculum fosters the notion that children can and should become participants and decision makers in their own learning, reversing the trend of school organizations systematically selecting out a growing number of students at an increasingly early age. Schools today are plagued with problems of behaviour management that often reach such a scale that classroom control takes precedent over instruction. Yet, as we saw in the example of The Alternate School, in Chapter 4, there have been examples of schools successfully turning these trends around. The central activity in the process has been full consultation with the students themselves. This has led to students "owning" and taking responsibility for the decisions they make, which in turn has led them to becoming accountable to each other for the implementation of their decisions. A recent example of these kinds of transformations comes from an elementary school in the UK. Frustrated with problems of classroom control and disruptive and aggressive behaviour, teachers, led by a very able head teacher, started a consultation process with students and parents. Over a number of years, they have collectively devised ways of improving self-esteem, sorting out problems, and agreeing upon rules and conventions for general behaviour based on positive reinforcement. Agreements can be modified through discussions and activities in the classroom at the daily circle time. Circle time activities include building self-esteem, learning listening skills, and building teamwork approaches. Children have been trained to intervene with their peers as "bully busters," "guardian angels," and mediation counselors (Highfield Junior School, 1997).

Finally, it is worth noting that some of the ideas and practices described above were first developed in less-developed countries as schools and their communities have sought to slough off the effects of elite, status-based education entrenched in a colonial past (Myers,1992). These **community development** ideas have now come full circle, informing the inclusive curriculum in our societies.

This multidisciplinary approach to education clearly has some potentially interesting effects. First, it deisolates the professionals so that teachers and schools become active in larger community networks of on-going dialogue and support. Second, it offers children more cooperative and less competitive strategies to problem solving and learning, and at the same time, a more accurate picture of the world they live in.

Although many educators would argue that classroom management becomes impossible for teachers when there is a wide range of ability in the classroom, in addition to the foregoing suggestions, there are relatively simple ways to organize schools and classrooms so that teachers are not overly burdened. The following final example is from a racially and ethnically mixed elementary school in Montreal where many of the children come from low-income families. As this example shows, when decisions are made in consultation with those affected, cooperation and change can follow.

Integrating Children with Learning Difficulties

Landpark School (a pseudonym for a school in Montreal) had two classes for grades five and six, averaging 24 students each. There was also one mixed grade five and six "special education" class made up of 10 students. The principal decided to try an informal experiment (a within-school plan, not officially approved by either the school board or the ministry). He consulted with the teachers and collectively they decided to give the experiment a try. Five "regular" classes were formed, each with less than 20 students. The students with the learning problems were distributed evenly among each class. Thus, the total number of students in the former four regular classes decreased, while the special education teacher's class increased; it became a regular class with a mix of students. The special education teacher remained available to assist the other teachers with the students who were designated as having special needs.

The teachers reported that the experiment was a huge success. What they liked most was the fact that the class sizes were reduced, making them more manageable. The presence of a few learning-disabled students in each class did not negate the benefits of the reduced class size. In addition, both the regular and the learning-disabled children benefited from being in an integrated setting. As one teacher stated, "now the learning disabled kids can't get away with things. The other kids in the class won't put up with nonsense. So they tow the line and are much better off for it." Another teacher remarked that the integrated setting represented the reality that the children would encounter in the world outside of school.

The teachers did not see the learning disabled students as "a problem." Rather, they saw these students' previous isolation as a problem and their integration into the regular classes as a large part of the solution to their special needs.

Source: Cleghorn, A., D'Amico, M., & Prochner, L. (1990).

Multicultural Education through Science Education

How can the school acknowledge the diversity of the school and the wider community? How can a school whose population is *not* diverse bring a multicultural dimension into the curriculum? (Peacock, 1992). An experiment carried out in England addressed these questions through a multicultural science curriculum at the primary school level. At the same time, problems relating to teachers' insecurity teaching science, the language and terminology of science, and teaching science to children for whom English is a second language were dealt with. The program was built on several ideas: first, that science is as related to culture as are art, music, or poetry; second, that teachers tend to hold traditional views of the nature of science that see science as something fixed and objective; and third, that there is considerable overlap between multicultural education, language development, and the processes of science education. Finally, the program was premised on an expanded definition of science, merging it with social science.

When the new multicultural approach was applied to lessons in which the topic was **antiracism,** children were asked to draw a scientist and then to describe what the scientist was doing. Their drawings were of white, middle-aged or older males in white coats. However, the children described what was going on in the pictures variously, for example, "as finding ways to destroy the earth," "turning lead to gold," or "finding a cure for cancer." That is, the children quickly learned that science has social, political, economic, and moral dimensions (Wyvill, 1992, p. 12). When such dimensions provide the framework for teaching science it becomes possible to expand the traditional view of science to include *different ways of looking, believing, and thinking.* This allows the teacher to draw children into a discussion of cultural and physical differences and similarities among the children themselves. Thus the scientific concept of *continuous variation* is easy to demonstrate in a multiracial classroom while teaching children about the basic scientifc method of observation. Children come to understand that while there may be physical differences among them, which may appear to be immense, the genetic differences are essentially insignificant. Children then come to know something about the way people attach social meaning to physical appearance and in turn they may gain insight into the nature of prejudices and the ways that stereotypes are formed.

In the same manner that the children themselves become a resource for teaching science, so too do the food, the plants, the music, the rituals, and the beliefs that are found in their homes. It is one thing to bring items from home for special ethnic or religious celebration days, it is another to find out what the chemistry is behind a flat chapathi and a leavened piece of French bread. Similarly, one can teach dissection procedures using a simple paring knife and an orange, an okra, or any other "exotic" vegetable. And in celebrating festivals the children themselves can teach their peers as well as the teacher what the different rituals and symbols mean. In such ways the classroom becomes a truly cooperative place to learn. In due course, children's critical skills may also be developed by teaching them to analyze quantitatively as well as qualitatively their own textbooks and computer and television programs for cultural bias as well as for elements of racism and sexism.

When teaching is inclusive in the above-described ways, it builds in the possibility of achieving many of the desired social as well as academic changes in schooling, such as increasing the access of girls and women to careers in science and technology. As Erwin and MacLennan (1994) point out, the current shortage of qualified people in science and technology renders the time right for implementing programs that attract women and other minorities. Although it is acknowledged that the problems of gender bias are systemic and change is needed in society as a whole, Gaskell, McLaren and Novogrodsky (1989), Young (1995), Secada (1989), and others suggest that changes must be made in the early schooling years. By intervening on traditional schooling and socialization patterns that perpetuate gender and other stereotypes, self images, and expectations, the social goals of education may be realized.

SUMMARY/CONCLUSIONS

In this chapter we have tried to show how the history of schooling has been marked by fairly constant efforts to bring about change that would benefit both the system of education and society as a whole. Often the vision has been idealistic and somewhat grandiose. Any plan to change the system is bound to encounter resistance and criticism, but is there any choice?

What is more important than grand schemes is to try to understand what the conditions are that allow for well thought-out changes to be implemented. We need also to understand why there appears to be so much enthusiasm for changes that are of the quick-fix type, and, at the same time, resistance to reforms that would truly increase equality. Why, for example, does it not seem likely that an inclusive curriculum will be adopted throughout an entire school system? The answer is both simple and complex. On the one hand, we all agree that there should be equality of educational opportunity for all. None of us would reasonably say that the poor or new Canadians or the disabled or ethnic minorities should be excluded from the mainstream. But that they are is evident from a quick glance at the still predominantly Anglo-Saxon names listed among the board of directors of some of Canada's largest corporations. This suggests that *access to positions of power* is strictly but subtly controlled. Part of this control starts when children are very young with parents who can afford to send their children to private schools where they will mix only with others from similar backgrounds. Friendships are formed among those who attend the same schools. Membership in nonformal associations follows the same kind of path. When applying for summer jobs or employment upon the completion of university, it helps to have personal contacts. Since there are only a few places at the top, few people are willing to open the doors wider. Power is a scarce resource.

There are many lessons that can be drawn from the accounts in this chapter. First, the context of change is crucial to its success or failure. There has to be a good reason to change—not just politicians' agendas. Second, teachers must be able to see the positive benefits of the change. Third, the way in which changes occur is crucial to successful innovation. We have much to learn from the mistakes and success of other countries. Fourth, the process of change is long and slow. Teachers cannot be rushed; they need time to reflect and adapt. Finally, teachers must be involved in the process, and the voices of the dissenters must be heard (Sanders, 1999, pp. 399–400).

KEY TERMS

antibias curriculum	deschooling	hands-on learning
antiracism	first language maintenance	home schooling
community development	free schools	inclusive curriculum

internal and external efficiency

needs assessment

open schools

policy of mulitculturalism

qualificationism

social change

sociotechnical system

status competition

total, early French immersion

transitional bilingual education

unity in diversity

DISCUSSION QUESTIONS

1. Identify differences in educational policy issues from one province to another. What might account for these differences?

2. What are the main debates in education in your community? How are these linked to perceptions of change that has already occurred or to people's ideas of changes that are desirable?

3. Use Norman Henchey's argument regarding classroom schooling in a technologically advanced society as the basis for a class debate. Defend either your support for or your opposition to his arguement.

RECOMMENDED READINGS/REFERENCES

Aikenhead, G. S.(1990). Scientific/technological literacy, critical reasoning, and classroom practice. In S. P. Norris, & L. M. Phillips (Eds.). *Foundations of literacy policy in Canada* (pp.127–146). Calgary: Detselig.

Bowles, S., & Gintis, H. (1976). *Schooling in capitalist America*. New York: Basic Books.

Buchbinder, H., & Newson, J. (1994). Corporate-university linkages in Canada: Transforming a public institution. In L. Erwin, & D. MacLennan (Eds.). *Sociology of education in Canada* (pp. 473–498). *Toronto*: Copp Clark Longman.

Canada (1982).The Canadian Charter of Rights and Freedoms. In Ghosh, R., & Ray, D. (Eds.). *Social change and education in Canada* (pp. 367–372). Toronto: Harcourt Brace Jovanovich.

Cleghorn, A., D'Amico, M., & Prochner, L. (1999). Teachers' views of elementary science in linguistically diverse school settings in Quebec. *Educational theory and practice*. Under review.

Cleghorn, A., & Genesee, F. (1984). Languages in contact: An ethnographic study of interaction in an immersion school. *TESOL Quarterly, 18*(4), 595–625.

Cleghorn, A., & Lowerison, G. (1991). *When minority becomes majority. Report of a study carried out in the South Shore Protestant School Board*. Unpublished monograph. Concordia University: Montreal.

Collins, R. (1979). *The credential society*. New York: Academic Press.

Derman-Sparks, L. and the A.B.C. Task Force. (1993). *The anti-bias curriculum: Tools for empowering young children*. Washington, D.C.: NAEYC.

Dore, R. (1976). *The diploma disease.* London: George Allen & Unwin Ltd.

Erwin, L., & MacLennan, D. (1994). *Sociology of education in Canada.* Toronto: Copp Clark Longman.

Fleming, R. W. (1990). The artifact as text: being literate in a technological society. In S. Norris, & L. M. Phillips, (Eds.), *Foundations of literacy policy in Canada.* (pp.53–68). Calgary: Detselig.

Fletcher, C. (1999). Nunavut EMBA Information Package. Department of Anthropology. St. Mary's University: Halifax.

Freebody, P., & Welch, A. R. (Eds.). (1993). *Knowledge, culture & power: International perspectives on literacy as policy and practice.* Pittsburgh: University of Pittsburgh Press.

Fukuyama, F. (1999). *The great disruption: Human nature and the reconstruction of social order.* New York: Profile Books.

Gaskell, J., McLaren, A. & Novogrodsky, M. (1989). Claiming an education: Feminism and Canadian schools. Toronto: Our schools/our selves.

Genesee, F. (1987). *Learning through two languages.* Cambridge: Newbury House Publishers.

Ghosh, R., & Ray, D. (Eds.). (1995). *Social change and education in Canada* (3rd ed.) Toronto: Harcourt Brace.

Hatch, A. (Ed.). (1995). *Qualitative research in early childhood settings.* Connecticut: Praeger.

Heneveld, W. (1994). Planning and monitoring the quality of primary education in sub-Saharan Africa. Technical Note No. 4. Washington, D.C.: World Bank.

Henchey, N. (1987). Communication technology and the transformation of learning. In R. Ghosh, & D. Ray (Eds.), *Social change and education in Canada* (pp. 37-58.). Toronto: Harcourt Brace.

Hern, M. (Ed.). (1996). *Deschooling our lives.* Philadelphia: New Society Publishers.

Highfield Junior School. (1997). *Changing our school: promoting positive behaviour.* London: Institute of Education, University of London.

Holt, J. (1982). *How children fail.* New York : Delta/Seymour Lawrence.

Hurn, C. J. (1993). *The limits and possibilities of schooling.* Toronto: Allyn and Bacon.

Illich, I. (1996). *Deschooling society.* London: Marion Boyars.

Lambert, W. & Tucker, G. R. (1972). *The bilingual education of children: The St. Lambert experiment.* Rowley, Massachusetts: Newbury House.

Meighan, R. (1997). T*he next learning system and why home-schoolers are trailblazers.* Nottingham, UK: Educational Heretics Press.

Mpofu, E. (1996). I am because we are. Presentation made at Concordia University in conjunction with the Concordia-University of Zimbabwe link, Montreal, April 16.

Myers, R. G. (1992). *The twelve who survive. New York: Routledge.*

Neill, A. (1960). *Summerhill: A radical approach to child rearing.* New York: Hart Publishing.

Norris, S. P., & Phillips, L. M. (1990). *Foundations of literacy policy in Canada.* Calgary, AB: Detselig.

Palmer, H. (1975). *Immigration and the rise of multiculturalism.* Vancouver: Copp Clark.

Peacock, A. (1992). *Science in primary schools: The multicultural dimension.* London: Routledge.

Porter, J. A. (1965) *The vertical mosaic.* Toronto: University of Toronto Press.

Sanders, M. (1999). *Implementing outcomes-based education in South Africa*: In *What lessons can science educators learn from classroom practitioners in New Zealand? Proceedings of the 7th annual conference of the Southern African Association for Research in Mathematics and Science Education.* Harare.

Secada, W. G (1989). *Equity in education.* Philadelphia: Falmer.

Seidman, K. (1999, May 12). Laptops or textbooks. *The Montreal Gazette.*

Serpell, R. (1993). *The significance of schooling.* Cambridge: Cambridge University Press.

Smith, D. S. (1993). *Home schooling in Canada.* Francombe Place Research Associates.

Welch, A. R., & Freebody, P. (1993). Explanations of the current international 'literacy crisis'. In P. Freebody, & A. R. Welch (Eds.). *Knowledge, culture and power. International perspectives on literacy as policy and practice* (pp. 6–22). Pittsburg: The Falmer Press.

Wynne, B. (1988). Classroom ideas for antiracism through science in primary education. In A. Peacock (Ed.), *Science in primary schools: The multicultural dimension* (pp. 11-27). London: Routledge.

Wyville, B. (1992). Classroom ideas for antiracism through science in primary education. In A. Peacock (Ed.). *Science in primary schools: The multicultural dimension* (pp.11–27). London: Routledge.

Young, J. R. (1995). Demographic changes and educational development. In R. Ghosh, & D. Ray (Eds), *Social change and education in Canada* (pp. 54–65).Toronto: Harcourt Brace Jovanovich.

Glossary

A

Acculturation (p. 4) The changes that occur in values, attitudes, and ways of behaving within a group through first-hand cultural contact. Socialization into a new culture.

Achieved status (p. 5) Social position (status) gained largely through one's own efforts.

Antibias curriculum (p. 122) A program that ensures equitable access, treatment, and results in education.

Antiracism (p. 125) Opposition to discrimination based on race.

Ascribed status (p. 5) Social position based on characteristics that are present from birth, such as race and sex.

B

Bureaucracy (p. 47) An organization that is set up to achieve specific goals with maximum efficiency.

C

Cause and effect (p. 19) A linear relationship in which one variable determines the other.

Centralized education system (p. 9) Control of the education system by the state.

Cognitive perspective on socialization (p. 94) A theory of learning and of development that emphasizes perceptions and thought.

Communal orientation (p. 109) A shared view in which the needs of the group or community are given priority over those of the individual.

Communicative competence (p. 59) The ability to use language effectively according to the particular situation (i.e., school, home).

Community development (p. 123) Practices that originate at the local level that contribute to the well-being of the group.

Conflict perspective (p. 5) A perspective that characterizes formal education as a system that contributes to social inequality. This approach emphasizes dominant class interests and how these are imposed on the lower and middle classes.

Conscientization (critical consciousness) (p. 74) Described by Freire as an awakening process that involves a reinterpretation of what is considered to constitute knowledge.

Constructivist model of teaching (p. 57) A child-centered view of learning that holds that each child constructs knowledge within themselves.

Controlled experiment (p. 19) Testing for the influence of particular factors on specific results.

Correspondence principle or theory (p. 31) The role of the school in reproducing the class system.

Critical pedagogy (p. 76) The study of the relationship between power and knowledge. Critical pedagogy asks how and why knowledge gets constructed, and what the social functions of knowledge are.

Critical theory (p. 34) A school of thought and a process of critique that claims that any critique must not hold to its own doctrinal assumptions but be self-critical.

Cultural capital (p. 30) The inherited values of one's group and/or social class (economic, cultural, social, and symbolic), reinforced in schools through curriculum and pedagogy.

Cultural deficit (p. 53) The perception that a student is disadvantaged due to their social status or cultural background.

Cultural diffusion (p. 4) The dissemination of a society's knowledge and culture.

Cultural production (p. 5) The role that higher education institutions play in producing new knowledge in technology, science, the social sciences, the humanities, business, art, and other areas.

Culture (p. 4) The ways of perceiving, thinking, believing, and behaving that characterize the members of a particular social group.

Culture contact (p. 4) The contact that occurs when members of one cultural group live in close proximity to members of another cultural group.

Culture of silence (p. 73) A culture of passivity, which is created in the classroom by teaching practices and curricula that stem from the power of the dominant class.

Custodial function (p. 8) The role of the school in looking after children during school hours.

D

Decentralized education system (p. 9) A system that is controlled by local authorities, the community, or parents.

Definition of the situation (p. 27) When a situation is defined as real it becomes real in its consequences.

Dependent variables (p. 19) The factor measured in an experiment that may change because of manipulation of the independent variable.

Deschooling (p. 117) The removal of education from a formal classroom setting.

Dialogue (p. 73) An approach to teaching that is characterized by cooperation and acceptance of interchange ability in the roles of teacher and learner.

Discursive practices (p. 39) Refers to what can be said and thought, by whom, when, and with what authority.

Diversity (p. 3) A society in which the members are of different ethnic backgrounds, races, cultures, or religions.

Division of labour (p. 5) The organization of economic activity into parts.

Dominant group (p. 4) The group that holds the most important and powerful positions in a society.

E

Educational goals (p.14) The stated purposes of a formal system of education.

Ego (p. 94) The I; that which thinks, feels and acts; the self.

Empowerment (p. 82) Refers to providing students with knowledge, skills, and values required to become social critics who can make and implement effective social, political and economic decisions.

Equality of educational opportunity (p. 6) Equal access to schooling, equal treatment within schools, and the potential for equal results.

F

Feminist pedagogy (p. 85) The study of how gendered knowledge and experience are produced and transmitted.

First language maintenance (p. 112) The continued use and development of a student's first language after the start of schooling in a second language.

First Nations people (p. 15) Canada's aboriginal population.

Formal curriculum (p. 61) The courses and subjects to be taught at each grade level as prescribed by those in charge of the education system.

Formal education (p. 2) The set of organized activities that are intended to transmit skills, knowledge, and values. (See informal and non-formal education.)

Formal organization (p. 46) A type of group or interaction system in which behaviour is directed towards specific goals.

Free schools (p. 114) Schools operated by parent and community groups according to a particular philosophy of childhood.

Functional perspective (p. 5) Theoretical view that sees education as a structure that contributes to the stability and equilibrium of society.

Functionally literate (p. 3) The ability to read, write, and calculate well enough to get along in one's society.

G

Gender inclusive curriculum (p. 86) A curriculum that includes the writings and life experiences of women; their accounts of and interpretations of history.

Generalized other (p. 95) A generalization based on what others think or do, acquired through socialization.

Generative themes (p. 82) Freire's notion that curriculum should include themes and social issues relevant to student life couched in student vocabulary, which can lead to reflection, action, and change.

Governance (p. 9) Control and operation of the education system.

H

Hands-on learning (p.118) Education program that combines classroom instruction with practical activity, often out of school.

Hidden curriculum (p. 61) Everything that is learnt by children in school but is not part of the formal curriculum (e.g., social norms relating to competition, achievement, and authority).

Home schooling (p. 117) Home-based education where instruction is provided by parents or members of the community.

I

I (p. 27) The individual's reaction to situations from his/her standpoint.

Id (p. 94) Term coined by Freud referring to the individual's biological or unconscious instincts that seek immediate gratification.

Ideal types (p. 27) A theoretical construct, first conceived by Max Weber, that delineates the prototypical characteristics of society's basic institutions.

In loco parentis (p. 8) Latin for "in the place of parents"; refers to the assumption of parent-like responsibility by the schools.

Inclusive curriculum (p. 122) Education that acknowledges the presence of all in society regardless of ability, ethnicity, religion, or intelligence.

Independent variables (p. 19) The manipulated, influential factor in an experiment. (See dependent variables.)

Individualistic orientation (p. 109) A shared view in which the needs of the individual are more important than those of the group.

Informal education (p. 2) Learning that takes place outside of school, through the process of social interaction.

Informal organization (p. 47) The patterns of interaction within a formal organization that emerge on the basis of social and other criteria.

Intended functions (p. 3) The planned results of an education system or policy.

Internal and external efficiency (p. 117) Terms that are used in education program evaluation to determine the effectiveness of a program in terms of both its functioning within and the cost-benefits to society.

Internalization (p. 93) A process by which individuals incorporate society's norms and expectations into their own minds.

Interpretive procedures (p. 32) Basic rules and procedures drawn upon by teachers when interacting with students and with each other in an educational setting.

Interpretive sociology (p. 27) Strain of sociology concerned with the perception of the nature of events and social interaction, and on meanings that are constructed and reconstructed in that process.

Interpretive theorists (p. 18) Researchers who view society as emerging from and maintained by social interaction.

Intersubjectivity (p. 96) Refers to the process in which individuals interpret the knowledge that they have accumulated through experience including the knowledge which has been transmitted by parents and teachers.

L

Legitimating ideology (p. 5) A sct of beliefs that justifies or supports the status quo.

Liberal feminism (p. 36) A perspective that is interested in the relationship between women and schooling.

M

Macro, mid, and micro levels of analysis (p. 17) Studies which focus on larger structural processes, mid-level institutional analysis, or small scale-analysis of social activity or social interaction (as in classrooms).

Male hegemony (p. 38) The worldview or power structure that is maintained by the dominant class (usually made up of men).

Me (p. 27) That part of the self which represents internalized social attitudes and expectations.

Melting pot (p. 100) A society or place where social and cultural assimilation occurs.

Mentoring (p. 96) A conscious relationship between an adult and student intended to provide general guidance and support to the student.

Meritocracy (p. 6) A system of stratification based on personal achievement.

Moral socialization (p. 99) The process of learning society's normative system, including the organization of injustice and inequality, which is passed on by schools.

N

Narratives (p. 54) Stories that tell of an individual's life experiences.

Needs assessment (p. 120) A study conducted to determine the requirements of a situation or group most in need of proposed changes.

Neo-Marxist theory (p. 29) Theory interested in the relationship between political and economic forces.

Non-formal education (p. 2) Organized education and instruction out of school (e.g., piano lessons, scouts).

Norms (p. 47) Social consensus governing beliefs, attitudes, and behaviour.

O

Open schooling (p. 114) Education within the regular system characterized by small-group instruction, sometimes in classrooms without walls.

Open-structured schools (p. 47) Schools that group students according to achievement or interest rather than age and grade.

Outcomes-based education (p. 115) A system of education or instruction that is guided by clearly defined desired results.

P

Participant structures (p. 60) The patterns of participation that emerge in schools and classrooms that are often tied to cultural factors.

Patriarchal ideology (p. 36) A set of beliefs held by a society that preserves the dominance and privileges of men in relation to women.

Pedagogy (p. 71) The production of knowledge, identities, and values.

Phenomenology (p. 33) Study of events that includes the meanings and interpretations of the participants.

Pluralism (p. 100) A society in which people of all races and cultures are distinct but may not have social parity.

Policy of multiculturalism (p. 110) Canada's policy to promote linguistic and cultural diversity within a bilingual context.

Political socialization (p. 99) The role of the school in teaching the values and norms that support the prevailing structure, including the dominant political ideology.

Post-modernist feminism (p. 39) A focus on the relationship between power and knowledge as defined by the dominant male perspective.

Praxis (p. 75) The combination of reflection and action.

Primary socialization (p. 93) Learning that takes place during the early years of a person's life through interaction with primary caregivers (usually parents).

Q

Qualificationism (p. 114) The increasing need for higher educational credentials to obtain employment.

Qualitative paradigm (p. 19) A research perspective that includes subjective interpretations of events and processes.

Quantitative paradigm (p. 19) A research perspective that relies on objective recording of events and on controlled experimentation.

R

Reflective practice (p. 58) An element of teacher education that involves analysis of teaching and ongoing plans for change in practice.

Resistance (p. 77) Group or individual behaviour that is antisocial and counter to the values of the dominant group.

S

Secondary socialization (p. 96) Socialization that occurs within the school through contact with peers, the media, and teachers.

Selection and allocation function (p. 7) The distribution of individuals into certain roles and positions based on social class, ethnicity, and other ascriptive criteria within the educational system.

Self (p. 27) An individual's notion of who he or she is.

Significant other (p. 95) Individuals who influence a child's development through constant interaction and through strong affective ties.

Social boundaries (p. 59) Characteristics and situations that define the differences between different social classes and groups.

Social change (p. 113) Evolution of society in responce to new conditions, for example, technical developments.

Social class (p. 2) An individual's position in society's hierarchy based on their possession of whatever criteria (e.g., education, income) are the most highly valued by the dominant class.

Social context (p. 3) The societal circumstances in which an event takes place.

Social control (p. 7) Social pressures that ensure compliance with established norms.

Social learning theory (p. 94) A theory of learning that emphasizes the role of social interaction and social context.

Social meaning (p. 59) The shared meanings attached to personal attributes, as in stereotyping.

Social mobility (p. 5) An individual's upward movement in society's hierarchical system.

Social process (p. 2) Sequence of activity driven by social interaction.

Social reconstructivist (p. 58) A model of teaching for social change that is antiracist, free of social class and gender distinctions.

Social stratification (p. 5) The system of organizing individuals and groups into a hierarchy based on society's values (e.g., education, income, occupation).

Social structure (p. 5) Society conceived of and organized as a unit distinct from the particular individuals who make it up.

Socialist feminism (p. 36) A division of feminism that sees women's oppression as related to gender relations as well as to capitalism.

Socialization (p. 93) The lifelong learning process through which individuals develop their sense of self and become part of the social group they live in.

Socially constructed (p. 95) The construction of situations by individuals interacting.

Sociotechnical system (p. 120) The subsector of society involving the use of technology.

Status competition (p. 114) Competition between different groups to achieve a higher social status.

Status culture (p. 30) A particular lifestyle such as language, dress code, association groups or interests that are deemed desirable by the dominant group in society.

Status groups (p. 27) A group of individuals who share similar values and lifestyles.

Structures of dominance (p. 33) The institutions and ideologies used by the dominant class to perpetuate and increase their advantaged position.

Superego (p. 94) The internalized culture and norms of society that govern an individual's socially acceptable behaviour

Symbolic interactionism (p. 32) A perspective focusing on how the self and social relationships develop through social experience and communication.

T

Taken for granted perspective (p. 99) Ideas and opinions that are presumed to be "normal."

Technological artefact (p. 120) The products of a technologically based society.

Technologically literate (p. 120) Knowledge and understanding of the role, functioning, and politics of the use of technology in society.

Theory of liberation (p. 72) A view that educational practice could and should be emancipatory for all.

Total, early French immersion (p. 112) Instruction in French only during the first years of schooling.

Tracking (p. 97) Process whereby teachers evaluate, classify, and place pupils into high-, middle-, or low-ability groups. This may result in separate classes for pupils with different levels of ability or the formation of ability groups within a single class

Transformative intellectual (p. 56) A person who is interested in uncovering the role of education in the struggle for power and meaning in society.

Transitional bilingual education (p. 112) Instruction in a second language for the purposes of replacing the first language. (See first language maintenance.)

Transmission model (p. 57) A set of methods or body of knowledge that is imparted directly from teacher to students.

Typification (p. 97) An interpretation and categorization of individuals on the basis of prior experience and "knowledge" of characteristics; standardized schemes of behaviour.

U

Unintended functions (p. 3) The unplanned but generally regular results of formal education.

Unity in diversity (p. 110) The notion that a society is strengthened and unified by maintaining the cultural diversity of its citizens. The fundamental goal of Canada's federal multicultural policy.

V

Voice (p. 82) Awareness and articulation of a person's conviction that they are active agents of change.

Voluntary minority (p. 15) An immigrant who has chosen to leave their native homeland in expectation of improving their own or their children's lives.

Weblinks

Chapter 1

http://www.oecd.org/statlist.htm#edu

This page from the Organization for Economic Cooperation and Development (OECD) offers international comparative data on key aspects of education systems from various countries.

http://www.cmec.ca

The home page of the Council of Ministers of Education (CMEC), the national voice for education in Canada, contains links to Canada's provincial ministries and departments of education. It also offers access to *Education Indicators in Canada*, published by the CMEC and Statistics Canada, and *Report on Education in Canada*, an overview of provincial and territorial initiatives in education.

http://www.unesco.org/education/educprog/stat/stat-idx.htm

This Web site from the Education Information Service of UNESCO provides data on education from their Statistical Yearbook.

http://www.statcan.ca/english/Pgdb/People/uducat/htm

This site from Statistics Canada offers data on the education status of Canadians.

Chapter 2

http://www.runet.edu/~lridener/DSS/DEADSOC.HTML

Don't be fooled by the seemingly irreverent name of this site. The *Dead Sociologists' Society* offers extensive information on the major historical figures in sociology.

Chapter 3

http://www.ericsp.org

The Educational Resources Information Center (ERIC) Clearinghouse on Teaching and Teacher Education is an electronic database of over 950,000 records of journal articles, research reports, curriculum and teaching guides, conference papers, and books.

http://www.umanitoba.ca/publications/cjeap

The *Canadian Journal of Educational Administration and Policy*, a peer reviewed electronic journal, publishes work that raises important questions and promotes debates on problems of educational practice and policy.

Chapter 4

http://www.lib.wmc.edu/pub/jcp/jcp.html

The *Journal of Critical Pedagogy* is a refereed electronic publication of research, articles, and sociocultural critiques that have implications for critical theory and cultural studies.

http://www.infed.org

The Informal Education Homepage provides information on the informal education movement as well as links to key books and web-based information on theorists who have influenced the movement, such as Paulo Freire.

Chapter 5

http://paradigm.soci.brocku.ca/~lward

George's Page, the official publication of the Mead Project at Brock University's Department of Sociology, is dedicated to republishing the work of George Herbert Mead on the Internet.

Chapter 6

http://www.pch.gc.ca/multi/html/english.html

The home page from Canada's Secretary of State for Multiculturalism provides links to information on Canada's Multiculturalism Policy and the Canadian Multiculturalism Act.

http://www.schoolnet.ca/

Sponsored by the Government of Canada, SchoolNet is designed to promote the effective use of information technology by helping schools and library connect to the Internet.

Bibliography

Acker, S. (1988). Teachers, gender and resistance. *British Journal of Sociology of Education, 9,* 307–322.

Aikenhead, G. S. (1990). Scientific/technological literacy, critical reasoning, and classroom practice. In S. P. Norris, & L. M. Phillips (Eds.), *Foundations of literacy policy in Canada* (pp.127–146). Calgary: Detselig.

Althusser, L. (1971). Ideology and ideological state apparatuses. In *Lenin and philosophy and other essays*. (B. Brewster, Trans.) (pp. 127–193). London: New Left Books.

Anderson, G. (1990). *Fundamentals of educational research*. New York: Falmer Press.

Apple, M. (1982). *Education and power*. Boston: Routledge and Kegan Press.

Apple, M. W., & Christian-Smith, L. K. (Eds.). (1991). *The politics of the textbook*. New York: Routledge.

Apple, M. W. (1979). *Ideology and curriculum*. Boston: Routledge Kegan Paul.

Arnot, M. (1994). Male hegemony, social class, and women's education. In L. Stone (Ed.), *The education feminist reader* (pp. 84–104). New York: Routledge.

Aronowitz, S., & Giroux, H. (1985). *Education under siege*. New York: Bergin & Garvey.

Aronowitz, S., & Giroux, H. (1993). *Education still under siege*. New York: Bergin & Garvey.

Ballantine, J. (1983). *The sociology of education: A systematic analysis*. New Jersey: Prentice-Hall.

Barakett, J., & Leonard, J. (1999, Fall). Resisting youth subcultures: Classroom practice and critical pedagogy. *Transformations: The Journal of Curriculum Transformation, 10*(2).

Barman, J. (1987). *Indian education in Canada*. Vancouver: University of British Columbia Press.

Baverstock-Angelus, D. (1999). Using teacher narratives for reflection, representation and reforms in teacher training programs. Unpublished M.A. thesis, Concordia University, Montreal.

Bélanger, P. W., & Rocher, G. (Eds.). (1975). *Ecole et societé au Québec*. Montreal: Hurtubise HMH.

Bernstein, B. (1973). *Call codes and control*. London: Routledge Kegan Paul.

Beyer, L. (1987). What knowledge is of most worth in teacher education? In J. Smyth (Ed.), *Educating teachers: Changing the nature of pedagogical knowledge*, (pp. 19–34). New York: Falmer Press.

Bibby, R., & Posterski, D. (1992). *Teen trends: A nation in motion.* Toronto: Stoddart.

Blau, P., & Scott, W. R. (1962). *Formal or-ganizations: A comparative approach.* San Fransisco: Chandler.

Bogdon, R. A., & Biklan, S. (1992). *Qualitative research for education: An introduction to theory and methods.* Boston: Allyn and Bacon.

Bourdieu, P., & Passeron, J. C. (1977). *Reproduction in education: Society and culture.* California: Sage.

Bourdieu, P. (1986). The forms of capital. In I. C. Richardson (Ed.), *Handbook of the-ory and research for the sociology of education.* (R. Nice, Trans.) (pp. 241–258). New York: Greenwood Press.

Bowles, S., & Gintis, H. (1976). *Schooling in capitalist America.* New York: Basic Books.

Brady, J. (1994). Critical literacy, feminism, and politics of representation. In C. Lankshear, & P. Mclaren (Eds.), *Politics of liberation: Paths from Freire* (pp.142–153). New York: Routledge.

Brock, C. (Ed.). (1996). *Global perspectives on teacher education. Oxford studies in comparative education.* Wallingford, Oxfordshire: Triangle.

Bruner, J. (1997). *The culture of education.* Massachusetts: Harvard University Press.

Buchbinder, H., & Newson, J. (1994). Corporate-university linkages in Canada: Transforming a public institution. In L. Erwin, & D. MacLennan (Eds.), *Sociology of education in Canada* (pp. 473–498). Toronto: Copp Clark Longman.

Canada (1982). The Canadian Charter of Rights and Freedoms. In R. Ghosh, & D. Ray (Eds.), *Social change and edu-cation in Canada* (pp. 367–372). Toronto: Harcourt Brace Jovanovich.

Cardinal, H. (1977). *The rebirth of Canada's indians.* Edmonton: Hurtig.

Carr, W., & Kemmis, S. (1983). *Becoming critical: Knowing through action re-search.* Victoria: Dean University.

Carrasco, R. L. (1981). Expanded aware-ness of student performance: A case study in applied ethnographic monitor-ing in a bilingual classroom. In H. Trueba, G. P. Guthrie, & K. H-P. Au (Eds.), *Culture and the bilingual class-room* (pp. 153–177). Rowley: Newbury House Publishers.

Cazden, C., & Hymes, D. (Eds.). (1972). *Functions of language in the classroom.* New York: Teachers College Press.

Clarke, B., & Trow, M. (1966). *The orga-nization context.* In T. Newcomb, & E. Wilson (Eds.), *College peer groups: Problems and prospects* (pp. 17–70). Chicago: Aldine.

Cleghorn, A., & Genesee, F. (1984). Languages in contact: An ethnographic study of interaction in an immersion school. *TESOL Quarterly, 18*(4), 595–625.

Cleghorn, A., D'Amico, M., & Prochner, L. (1999). Teachers' views of primary science in linguistically diverse settings in Quebec. *Curriculum and Teaching 14 (1)*, 95–100.

Cleghorn, A., & Lowerison, G. (1991). *When minority becomes majority.* Report of a study carried out in the South Shore Protestant School Board, Montreal. Unpublished monograph, Concordia University, Montreal, PQ.

Cleghorn, A., Mtetwa, D., Dube, R., & Munetsi, C. (1998). Classroom language use in multilingual settings: Mathematics lessons from Quebec and Zimbabwe. *Qualitative Studies in Education, 11*(3), 463–477.

Clement, W. (1975). *The Canadian corporate elite: An analysis of economic power*. Toronto: McClelland & Stewart.

Coleman, J. (1961). *The adolescent society*. New York: Free Press.

Coleman, J. (1966). The concept of equality of opportunity. *Harvard Educational Review*, 38, 7–32.

Collins, R. (1977). Functional and conflict theories of educational stratification. *American Sociological Review*, 36(6), 1002–19.

Collins, R. (1979). *The credential society*. New York: Academic Press.

Cooley, C. H. (1956). *Human nature and the social order*. Glencoe, IL: Free Press.

Corwin, R. G. (1965). *A sociology of education*. New York: Appleton-Century Crofts.

Crago, M., Annahatak, B., & Ningiuruvik, L. (1993). Changing patterns of language socialization in Inuit homes. *Anthropology and Education Quarterly*, 24(3), 205–223.

Culley, M., & Portuges, C. (1985). *Gendered subjects: The dynamics of feminist teaching*. Boston: Routledge & Keegan Paul.

De Castell, S. (1990). Defining significant knowledge: Some limits to literacy. In S. P. Norris, & L. M. Phillips (Eds.), *Foundations of literacy policy in Canada* (pp. 23–36). Calgary: Detselig.

Dei, G. (1996). Black/African-Canadian students' perspectives on school racism. In M. I. Alladin (Ed.), *Racism in Canadian schools* (pp. 42–57). Toronto: Harcourt Brace.

Delgado-Gaitan, C., & Trueba, H. (1991). *Crossing cultural borders: Education for immigrant families in America*. New York: Falmer Press.

Derman-Sparks, L., & the A.B.C. Task Force. (1993). *The Anti-bias curriculum: Tools for empowering young children*. Washington, DC: NAEYC.

Diamond, I., & Quinby, L. (Eds.). (1988). *Feminisms and Foucault: Reflections on resistance*. Boston: Northwestern University Press.

Dickinson, G. (1987). The legal dimensions of teachers' duties and authority. In R.Ghosh, & D. Ray, (Eds.), *Social change and education in Canada* (pp. 210–230). Toronto: Harcourt Brace Jovanovich.

Dore, R. (1976). *The diploma disease*. London: George Allen & Unwin.

Dreeben, R. (1968). *On what is learned in school*. Reading, MA: Addison –Wesley.

Durkheim, E. (1956). *Education and society*. Glencoe, IL: The Free Press.

Durkheim, E. (1961). *Moral socialization*. New York: The Free Press.

Ellsworth, E. (1990) Why doesn't this feel empowering? Working through repressive myths and critical pedagogy. In C. Luke, & J. Gore (Eds.), *Feminisms and critical pedagogies* (pp. 90–119). New York: Routledge.

Erwin, L., & MacLennan, D. (1994). *Sociology of education in Canada.* Toronto: Copp Clark Longman.

Fleming, R. W. (1990). The artifact as text: Being literate in a technological society. In S. P. Norris, & L. M. Phillips (Eds.), *Foundations of literacy policy in Canada* (pp.53–68). Calgary: Detselig.

Fletcher, C. (1999). *Nunavut EMBA information package.* Halifax: Department of Anthropology, St. Mary's University.

Flores, B., Cousin, P., & Dias, E. (1991). Transforming deficit myths about learning language and culture. *Language Arts, 68,* 369–379.

Fox-Genovese, E. (1986). Gender, race, class, canon. *Salmagundi: A quarterly of the humanities & social sciences, 72,* 131–143.

Freebody, P., & Welch, A. R. (Eds.). (1993). *Knowledge, culture & power: International perspectives on literacy as policy and practice.* Pittsburgh: University of Pittsburgh Press.

Freire, P. (1968). *Pedagogy of the oppressed.* New York: Seabury Press.

Freire, P. (1973). *Education for critical consciousness.* New York: Seabury Press.

Freire, P. (1985). *The politics of education: Culture, power and liberation.* Boston: Bergin and Garvey.

Fukayama, F. (1999). The great disruption: Human nature and the reconstruction of social order. New York: Profile Books.

Fullan, M., & Stiegelbauer, S. (1991). *The new meaning of educational change.* Toronto: OISE Press.

Fuller, B., & Snyder, C. W. (1991). Vocal teachers, silent pupils: Life in Botswana classrooms. *Comparative Education review, 35*(2), 274–294.

Fukuyama, F. (1999). *The great disruption: Human nature and the reconstruction of social order.* New York: Profile Books.

Gaskell, J. (1992). *Gender matters from school to work.* Toronto: OISE Press.

Gaskell, J., McLaren, A., & Novogrodsky, H. (1989). *Claiming and education: Feminism and Canadian schools.* Toronto: Education Foundation.

Genesee, F. (1987). *Learning through two languages.* Cambridge: Newbury House Publishers.

Ghosh, R. & Ray, D. (Eds.). (1987). *Social change and education in Canada* (1st. ed.). Toronto: Harcourt Brace Jovanovich.

Ghosh, R., & Ray, D. (Eds.). (1995). *Social change and education in Canada* (3rd ed.) Toronto: Harcourt Brace.

Gibson, M. A., & Ogbu, J. U. (Eds.). (1991). *Minority status and schooling.* New York: Garland Publishing.

Giroux, H., & McLaren, P. (1994). *Between borders.* New York:Routledge.

Giroux, H., & Simon, R. (1989). Popular culture and critical pedagogy: Everyday life as a basis for curriculum knowledge. In H. Giroux, & P. McLaren (Eds.),

Cultural pedagogy, the state and cultural struggle. (pp. 236–292) New York: State University of New York Press.

Giroux, H. (1983). *Theory and resistance in education.* Massachusetts: Bergin and Garvey.

Giroux, H. (1992) *Border crossings.* New York: Routledge.

Giroux, H. (1996). *Fugitive cultures: Race, violence and youths.* England: Routledge.

Goodlad, J. (1990). *Teachers for our nation's schools.* San Fransisco: Jossey-Bass.

Gordon, R. (1997). Structural adjustment and women in Zimbabwe: Effects and prospects. *Canadian Journal of Development Studies, XVIII*(2), 263–278.

Gore, J. (1992) Feminist politics in radical pedagogy, In C. Luke, & J. Gore (Eds.), *Feminisims and critical pedagogies* (pp. 25-53). New York: Routledge.

Gore, J. (1993). *The struggle for pedagogies.* New York: Routledge.

Gramsci, A. (1971). *Selections from the prison notebooks.* (Ed. and trans.) Q. Hoare & G. Nowell-Smith. New York: International Publishers.

Greenberger, E., & Sorensen, A. (1970). Interpersonal choices among a junior high school faculty. *Sociology of Education, 44,* 198–216.

Grimmett, P. P., & Wideen, M.(Eds.). (1995). *Changing times in teacher education.* London: Falmer Press.

Gumperz, J. J. (1986). Interactional sociolinguistics in the study of schooling. In J. Cook-Gumperz (Ed.), *The social construction of literacy* (pp. 45–68). Cambridge: Cambridge University Press.

Habermas, J. (1968) *Knowledge and human interests.* Boston: Beacon Press.

Hargreaves, D. H., Hester, S. K., & Mellor, F. J. (1975). *Deviance in classrooms.* London: Routledge and Keegan Paul.

Hatch, A. (Ed.). (1995). *Qualitative research in early childhood settings.* Connecticut: Praeger.

Heap, J. L. (1990). Effective functioning in daily life: A critique of concepts and surveys of functional literacy. In S.P. Norris, & L. M. Phillips (Eds.), *Foundations of literacy policy in Canada.* (pp. 37–52). Calgary: Detselig.

Henchey, N. (1987). Communication technology and the transformation of learning. In R. Ghosh, & D. Ray (Eds.), *Social change and education in Canada* (pp. 37-58.). Toronto: Harcourt Brace.

Heneveld, W. (1994). *Planning and monitoring the quality of primary education in sub-Saharan Africa.* Technical Note No. 4. Washington, DC: World Bank.

Hern, M. (Ed.). (1996). *Deschooling our lives.* Philadelphia: New Society Publishers.

Highfield Junior School. (1997). *Changing our school: Promoting positive behaviour.* London: Institute of Education, University of London.

Holmes Group (1986). *Tomorrow's teachers.* East Lansing: Holmes Group.

Holt, J. (1982). *How children fail.* New York: Delta/Seymour Lawrence.

Hurn, C. J. (1993). *The limits and possibilities of schooling.* Toronto: Allyn and Bacon.

Illich, I. (1996). *Deschooling society.* London: Marion Boyars.

Jackson, P. (1968). *Life in classrooms.* New York: Holt, Rinehart & Winston.

Jaenen, C., & Conrad, M. (1993). *History of the Canadian peoples.* Mississaauga, ON: Copp, Clark, Pitman.

Kessen, W. (1979). The American child and other cultural inventions. *American Psychologist, 34*, 815–820.

Laird, S. (1988). Reforming 'women's true profession': A case for 'feminist pedagogy' in teacher education? *Harvard Educational Review, 58*(4), 449–463.

Lambert, W., & Tucker, G. R. (1972). *The bilingual education of children: The St. Lambert experiment.* Rowley, MA: Newbury House.

Levin, B., & Young, J. (1994). *Understanding Canadian schools: An introduction to educational administration.* Toronto: Harcourt Brace.

Lewis, M. (1992). Interrupting patriarchy: Politics, resistance and transformation in the feminist classroom. In C. Luke, & J. Gore (Eds.), *Feminisms and critical pedagogies* (pp. 167-191). New York: Routledge.

Lindsay, B. (1990). Educational equity in cross-national settings. In M. Thomas (Ed.*), International comparative education: Practices, issues, and prospects* (pp. 197-226). New York: Pergamon.

Lipka, J. (1991). Toward a cutlurally based pedagogy: A case study of one Yup'ik Eskimo teacher. *Anthropology and Education Quarterly, 22,* 203–223.

Liston, D., & Zeichner, K. (1991). *Teacher education and the social conditions of schooling.* New York: Routledge.

Liston, D., & Zeichner, K. (1987). Critical pedagogy and teacher education. *Journal of education, 169*(3), 117–137.

Livingstone, D. W. (1983). *Class, ideologies and educational futures.* London: Routledge.

Livingstone, D. W. (1985). *Social crisis and school.* Toronto: Garamond Press.

Livingstone, D. W. (1994). Searching for missing links: Neo-Marxist theories of education. In L. Irwin, & D. MacLennan (Eds)., *Sociology of education in Canada: Critical perspectives in theory, research and practice* (pp. 55–82). Toronto: Copp Clark Longman.

Lortie, D. (1975). *Schoolteacher.* Chicago: University of Chicago Press.

Luke, C. & Gore, J. (1992). *Feminisims and critical pedagogies.* New York: Routledge.

MacDonald, M. (1980) Socio-cultural reproduction and women's education. In R. Deem. (Ed.), *Schooling for women's work* (pp.13–25). Boston: Routledge and Kegan Paul.

Mackie, M. (1987). *Constructing women and men.* Toronto: Holt, Rinehardt & Winston.

Mackie, M. (1994). Socialization. In R. Hagedorn (Ed.), *Sociology* (5th. ed.) (pp. 89–120). Toronto: Harcourt Brace and Company.

Magnuson, R. (1980). *A brief history of Quebec education*. Montreal: Harvest House.

Martell, G. (Ed.). (1974). *The politics of the Canadian public school*. Toronto: James Lorimer.

Martin, J. R. (1985). *Reclaiming a conversation: The ideal of the educated woman*. New Haven, CN: Yale University Press.

Martin, W. B. W. (1975). The negotiated order of teachers in team teaching situations. *Sociology of Education, 48,* 202–222.

Martin, W. B. W. (1976). *The negotiated order of the school*. Toronto: MacMillan.

Martin, W. B. W., & Macdonell, A. (1978). *Canadian education*. Toronto: Prentice Hall.

McLaren, P., & Lankshear, C. (Eds.). (1994). *Politics of liberation: Paths from Freire*. New York:Routledge.

McLaren, P. & Leonard, P. (1993). *Paulo Freire: A critical encounter. New York: Routledge.*

McLaren, P. (1995) *Critical pedagogy and predatory culture*. New York: Routledge.

McLaren, P. (1998). *Life in schools: An introduction to critical pedagogy in the foundations of education (3rd. ed.)*. Don Mills: Langerman.

Mead, G. H. (1934). *Mind, self and society*. Chicago: University of Chicago Press.

Meighan, R. (1997). *The next learning system and why home-schoolers are trailblazers*. Nottingham, UK: Educational Heretics Press.

Mifflen, F, & Mifflen, S. (1982). *The sociology of education*. Calgary: Detselig.

Mpofu, E. (1996). I am because we are. Presentation made at Concordia University in conjunction with the Concordia-University of Zimbabwe link, Montreal, April 16.

Murphy, R. (1979). *Sociological theories of education*. Toronto: McGraw-Hill Ryerson.

Myers, R. G. (1992). *The twelve who survive*. New York: Routledge.

Nathanson, M. (1970). Phenomenology and typification: A study in the philosophy of Alfred Schutz. *Social Research, 37,* 3–4, 6–8.

National Centre for Education Statistics. (1994). Washington: United States.

Neill, A. (1960). *Summerhill: A radical approach to child rearing*. New York: Hart.

Nelsen, R., & Nock, D. (Eds). (1978). *Reading, writing and riches: Education and the socio-economic order in North America*. Kitchener, ON: Between the Lines.

Norris, S. P., & Phillips, L. M. (1990). *Foundations of literacy policy in Canada*. Calgary, AB: Detselig.

Nunn, E.J., & Boyatzis, C. J. (1998/99). *Child growth and development*. Guilford, CN: McGraw-Hill.

Ogbu, J. U. (1991). Low school performance as an adaptation: The case of Blacks in Stockton, California. In M. A. Gibson, & J. U. Ogbu (Eds*.), Minority status and schooling* (pp. 249–286). New York: Garland Publishing.

Organization for Economic Cooperation and Development. (1996). *Education at a glance: OECD indicators.* Centre for Education Research and Innovation: Indicators of Educational Systems. Paris: OECD Publications Service.

Orpwood, G., & Garden, R. A. (1998) (Eds.). *Assessing mathematics and science literacy. TIMMS Monograph Series #4.* Vancouver: Pacific Educational Press.

Palmer, H. (1975). *Immigration and the rise of multiculturalism.* Vancouver: Copp Clark.

Parsons, T. (1967) The school class as a social system. In P. Rose (Ed.), *The study of society* (pp. 647–665). New York: Random House.

Peacock, A. (1992). *Science in primary schools: The multicultural dimension* London: Routledge.

Persell, C. H. (1977). *Education and inequality.* New York: The Free Press.

Phillips, S. U. (1972). Participant structures and communicative competence: Warm Springs children in community and classroom. In C. Cazden, V. John, & D. Hymes, D. (Eds.), *Functions of language in the classroom* (pp. 370–394). New York: Teachers College Press.

Porter, J. (1965). *The vertical mosaic: An analysis of social class and power in Canada.* Toronto: University of Toronto Press.

Prophet, R. B., & Rowell, P. M. (1993). Coping and control: Science teaching strategies in Botswana. *International Journal of Qualitative Studies in Education, 6*(3), 197–209.

Rich, A. (1980). *On lies, secrets and silences.* London: Virago.

Sanders, M. (1999). *Implementing outcomes-based education in South Africa: What lessons can science educators learn from classroom practitioners in New Zealand?* In *proceedings of the 7th annual conference of the Southern African Association for Research in Mathematics and Science Education.* Harare, Zimbabwe.

Schön, D. (1983). *The reflective practitioner.* London: Temple Smith.

Schutz, A. (1973). *Collected Papers: The problem of social reality (Vol. 1).* The Hague: Martinus Nijhoff.

Secada, W. G (1989). *Equity in education.* Philadelphia: Falmer.

Seidman, K. (1999, May 12). Laptops or Textbooks? *The Gazette.*

Serpell, R. (1993). *The significance of schooling.* Cambridge: Cambridge University Press.

Sheehan, N., & Fullan, M. (1995). Teacher education in Canada: A case study of British Columbia and Ontario. In M. Widden, & P. Grimmett (Eds.), *Changing times in teacher education* (pp. 89–101). Bristol: Falmer Press.

Shor, I. (1988). *Freire for the classroom: A sourcebook for liberatory teaching.* Portsmouth: Bayton/Cook.

Shor, I. (1992). *Empowering education: Critical teaching for social change.* Chicago: University of Chicago Press.

Shor, I. (1993). Education is politics: Paulo Freire's critical pedagogy. In P. McLaren, & P. Leonard (Eds.), *Paulo*

Freire: A critical encounter (pp. 25–35). New York: Routledge.

Short, J. (1968). *Gang delinquency and delinquent subcultures.* New York: Harper and Row.

Shrewsbury, C. M. (1987). What is feminist pedagogy? *Women's Studies Quarterly, 15*(3–4), 6–14.

Simon, R. (1987, April). Empowerment as a pedagogy of possibility. *Language Arts, 64*(4), 370–382.

Slavin, R. E. (1991). *Educational psychology: Theory into practice.* Engelwood Cliffs, New Jersey: Prentice-Hall.

Sleeter, C. E., & Grant, C. A. (1993). *Making choices for multicultural education.* Toronto: Maxwell Macmillan Canada.

Smith, D. (1987). *The everyday world as problematic: A feminist sociology.* Toronto: University of Toronto Press.

Smith, D. S. (1993). Home schooling in Canada. Francombe Place Research Associates.

Smyth, J. (1989). A critical pedagogy of classroom practice. *Journal of curriculum studies, 21(6),* 483–502.

Spencer, M. (1979). *The foundations of modern sociology.* (2nd ed.). Englewood Cliffs. NJ: Prentice-Hall.

Stairs, A. (1991). Learning processes and teaching roles in native education: Cultural base and cultural brokerage. *Canadian Modern Language Review. 47*(2), 280–294.

Statistics Canada. (1993).Aboriginal Data, Document 94-327. Ottawa: Canada.

Stigler, J. W., & Stevenson, H. W. (1998/99). How Asian teachers polish each lesson to perfection. In E. J. Nunn, & C. J. Boyatzis*, Child growth and development* (pp. 90-101). Guilford, Connecticut: McGraw-Hill.

Tabulawa, R. (1998). Teachers' perspectives on classroom practice in Botswana: Implications for pedagogical change. *International Journal of Qualitative Studies in Education 11*(2), 249–268.

Thomas, R. M. (Ed.). (1990). *International comparative education: Practices, issues and prospects.* New York: Pergamon.

Tom, A. (1987). Replacing pedagogical knowledge with pedagogical questions. In J. Smyth (Ed.), *Educating teachers: Changing the nature of pedagogical knowledge* (pp. 9–17). Philedelphia, PA: Falmer Press,

Tom, A. (1995). Stirring the embers: Reconsidering the structure of teacher education programs. In M. Wideen, & P. Grimmet (Eds.), *Changing times in teacher education* (pp. 117–131). Bristol: Falmer Press.

Trueba, H., Guthrie, G. P., & Au Hu-Pei, K. (1981). *Culture and the bilingual classroom.* Rowley: Newbury House Publishers.

Tulasiewicz, W. (1996). Is there a crisis in teacher education? In C. Brock (Ed.), *Global perspectives on teacher education*: *Oxford studies in comparative education* (pp. 19–34). Wallingford, Oxfordshire: Triangle.

UNICEF (1994). *Children and women in Zimbabwe: A situation analysis.* Harare: UNICEF.

Wagner, H. (Ed.). (1970). *Alfred Schutz on phenomenology and social relations.* Chicago: University of Chicago Press.

Weber, M. (1947). *The theory of social and economic organization.* New York: The Free Press.

Weber, S., & Mitchell, C. (1995). *That's funny, you don't look like a teacher!: Interrogating images and identity in popular cultures.* Washington DC: Falmer Press

Weiler, K., & Mitchell, C. (Eds.). (1992). *What schools can do: Critical pedagogy and practices.* New York: State University of New York Press.

Weiler, K. (1988). *Women teaching for change: Gender, class and power.* Massachusetts: Garvey Publishers.

Weiler, K. (1991). Freire and a feminist pedagogy of difference. *Harvard Educational Review,16*(4), 449–475.

Welch, A. R., & Freebody, P. (1993). Explanations of the current international 'literacy crisis'. In P. Freebody, & A. R. Welch (Eds.), *Knowledge, culture and power: International perspectives on literacy as policy and practice* (pp. 6–22). Pittsburg: The Falmer Press.

Werner, W. (1987). Curriculum and socialization. In R. Ghosh, & D. Ray (Eds.), *Social change and education in Canada.* (1st. ed.) (pp. 91–101). Toronto: Harcourt Brace.

Werner, W. (1995). Persistent curriculum issues. In R. Ghosh, & D. Ray (Eds.), *Social change and education in Canada (3rd. ed.)* (pp. 126–136). Toronto: Harcourt Brace.

Willis, P. (1977*). Learning to labour.* New York: Columbia University Press.

Wolpe, A. M. (1978). Education and the sexual division of labour. In A. Kuhn, & Wolpe, A. M. (Eds.), *Feminism and materialism* (pp. 290-328). Boston: Routledge and Kegan Paul.

Wolpe, A. M. (1988). *Within school walls.* New York: Routledge.

Wotherspoon, T. (Ed.). (1987). *The Political economy of Canadian schooling.* Toronto: Methuen.

Wotherspoon, T (1998). *The sociology of education in Canada: Critical perspectives.* Toronto: Oxford University Press.

Wynne, B. (1988). Classroom ideas for antiracism through science in primary education. In A. Peacock (Ed.), *Science in primary schools: The multicultural dimension* (pp. 11-27). London: Routledge.

Wyville, B. (1992). Classroom ideas for antiracism through science in primary education. In A. Peacock (Ed.), *Science in primary schools: The multicultural dimension* (pp.11–27). London: Routledge.

Young, J. R. (1995). Demographic changes and educational development. In R. Ghosh, & D. Ray (Eds.), *Social change and education in Canada* (pp. 54–65). Toronto: Harcourt Brace Jovanovich.

Index